Essential Tips for Woodcarvers

Guild of Master Craftsman Publications Ltd

This collection first published in 1997 by
Guild of Master Craftsman Publications Ltd,
Castle Place, 166 High Street, Lewes,
East Sussex BN7 1XU

ISBN 1 86108 055 7

Front cover photograph by Anthony Bailey
Illustrations by Simon Rodway

Designed by Derek Lee

Printed and bound in Great Britain
by Ebenezer Baylis & Son Ltd

Contents

Introduction 1

Section 1

Tools and Equipment

Mallet 3

Dentists' Tools 3

Motor Mounting 4

Residual Safety 4

For Eyes 4

Plastic Thumb Shield 5

Less Noise 5

Chisels from Knives 5

Boxed Set 6

Switch Protection 6

Fearsome Ferrules 6

Rounder the Better 7

Saw Point 7

Bow-saw Blades 7

Undercut Idea 8

Depth Gauge 8

Rasps and Rifflers 9

Fingerstall Thumb Shield 10

Hand Mallet 10

Key Tool 11

Shave Hook Scraper 11

Awkward Corners 12

Colour Coded Handles 12

Bendy Blades 13

Mini Gouges 14

Leather Guards 14

Profile Gauge 15

Finger Guards 15

Section 2

SHARPENING

Sharpening V-Tools 17

Polish Flutes 17

Section 3

TECHNIQUES

Letter Ideas 19

Lettering Layout 19

Hollow Hint 19

Tracing Film 19

Tracing Figures 20

Faster Cut 21

Card Cutout 21

Repeat Panels 21

Bench Height 21

Cheap Shaping 21

Extra Bench 22

Glue Guide 22

Hot-Melt Glue 23

Sanding Jig for Thin Leaves 23

Banish Zits 24

Cover Up 24

A Light Touch 25

Avoid Breakage 25

Push and Pull Cuts 25

Section 4

CLAMPS AND WORKHOLDERS

Modified Workholder 27

Tough Workholder 27

Painting Project 28

On the Mat 28

Toe-hold 29

Tough Gallows 30

Dogged Idea 31

Tommy Restraint 32

Press Workholder 32

Clamp Aid 33

Workmate Wonder 33

Carvers' Screw 34

Simple Support 35

Crafty Clamping 35

Simple Clamping 36

Holding Relief 36

Cheap Clamp 37

Portable Work centre 38

Section 5

WOOD

Woodworm Trap 39

Hiding Cracks 39

Bargain Boards 39

Waste Wood 39

Keep it Covered 40

Section 6

SANDING

Drum Sander 41

Sanding Tip 41

Sanding Flat 42

Softer Sanding 42

Handy Sander 42

Flexible Sanders 43

Section 7

GENERAL TIPS

Warmer Workshop 45

Paper Pointer 45

Old Gloves 45

Filing 46

Spot Fakes 46

Pack a Purse 46

Lap Board 47

Index 48

INTRODUCTION

Woodworking is a lifelong learning experience. Two adages are equally applicable to the craft: 'You're never too old to learn' and 'You learn something new every day'. The tips which readers send in to *Woodcarving* are excellent examples of just how apt they are.

These tips can be new ideas, old ideas re-assessed and improved, or improvisations and lash-ups. All are equally relevant.

Few woodworkers are rich enough to indulge their fancies, but most are ingenious and all are practical. The tips that fill this book are the natural result of this combination – lack of funds, as well as necessity, being the mother of invention.

Other than ingenuity, these tips and ideas demonstrate the willingness of woodworkers to exchange ideas. There is little talk of trade secrets, but a generous interchange, usually leading to more ideas and improvements.

Despite the fact that wood is man's oldest craft material, with a longer history than any other, the tips here prove we are still finding out new ways of using it. There is always something new for us all to learn from each other.

I hope you find some of the ideas here useful.

Neil Bell, Managing Editor,
Woodcarving *and* Woodturning *magazines*

SECTION 1
TOOLS AND EQUIPMENT

MALLET

Good carving mallets are expensive. As a professional woodcarver the mallet I normally use is made from an offcut of square beech (55mm, 2¼in square) with a handle turned on one end.

Admittedly a square mallet is harder to use when carving than a round one, but that is what was in the scrap box on the day I needed a mallet. A piece of 75mm, 3in square timber would have been better – I would have needed a much shorter head to achieve a useful weight. A lathe was used to form the handle, but a drawknife could have done the job as well.

Another mallet that I use in tight corners, is a length of old copper water pipe with a one-way valve on the end. It has a good weight and is small enough to be used in deep carvings without damaging the surrounding wood.

Given limitless resources I would buy the best of all tools, including a mallet. But, being realistic, I find that a free mallet and a good gouge is a better investment than an expensive mallet and a cheap gouge.

Rod Naylor

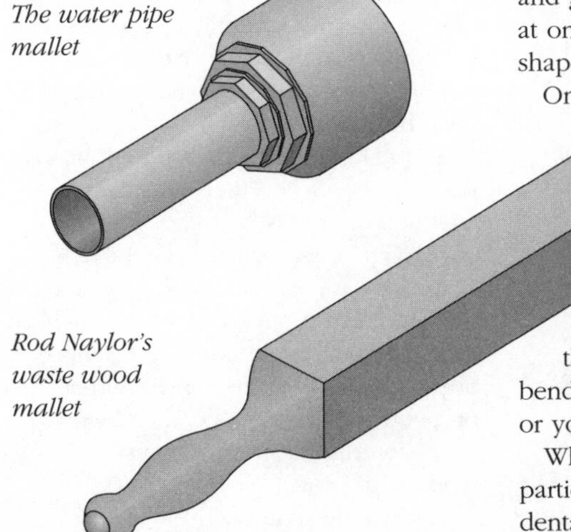

The water pipe mallet

Rod Naylor's waste wood mallet

DENTISTS' TOOLS

After reading about using dentists' drills for woodcarving, I thought I'd better tell you about dentists' hand tools. I have quite a collection of these tools: tiny 1.6mm, 1/16in, chisels, 3.1mm, 1/8in, chisels and gouges, and riffler files 1.6mm, 1/16in, at one end and 2.4mm, 3/32in, at the other shaped for working inside holes.

One tool, to push filling material into a hole, is bent at a 45° angle. I have sharpened this into a nice chisel for undercutting. There are many other detail tools that could be adapted. The steel in these tools is very good but they are quite brittle – don't try to bend them without softening with heat or you will snap them.

When I am doing relief carvings in particular I would be lost without my dental tool kit. I am fortunate in having ➢

a co-operative dentist who, when asked if he had any old tools, came out with a box full of them. My friends have not found their dentists to be as helpful.

Name not supplied

Motor Mounting

A common problem with flexible shaft carving machines is damage to the flexible shaft due to it catching in the wood or clothing.

I use the simple expedient of using a swivel with a snap hook to hang the motor on. These swivels with hooks are used by anglers and are available in a range of sizes. This method of mounting completely avoids the shaft damage that can occur on start-up. But, be careful as a deep catch could set the motor case spinning, making it difficult to switch off.

W.H.C. Brown

Residual Safety

As a safety measure, I plug all my power tools in through a residual current breaker mounted on a board at the end of an extension cable. Wired to the current breaker is a panic switch and I have enlarged the size of the switch with a large piece of plywood, painted bright red.

Residual current breaker

This combination of current breaker and panic switch means that I have no worries about accidentally cutting through the jigsaw's cable, or struggling to find the off switch when something is starting to go wrong.

Rod Naylor

For Eyes

Here is a tip to help older carvers (like me) when working on fine detail.

I have worn glasses for years and now use bifocals, which are perfect for normal use. In latter years I had to remove my glasses and hold the work very close to my eyes – a matter of 50-75mm, 2-3in, – to see details clearly. This was dangerous and impractical.

To solve the problem I bought a pair of very cheap reading glasses of the highest magnification available. Make sure that you buy them with the largest frame you can as the trick is to wear them over your usual pair.

You can get these reading glasses in various outlets 'off the peg'. Mine came from a newsagents shop and cost £5.00. The plastic lenses are light in weight and you should try them on over your normal specs before you buy as they must be a comfortable fit.

At first I felt a bit silly wearing two pairs of glasses together, especially if anyone saw me. Now I have four pairs of reading glasses scattered about the house, to save me having to fetch them from room to room when I need them. I have one pair by my knitting machine, one by the sewing machine, another pair where I do my general craftwork and a fourth pair in my carving workshop.

Normally, of course, I rely on my

bifocals, but I find my extra glasses invaluable when carving detail, threading needles and doing other fine craftwork such as embroidery. This tip could be of assistance to carvers and husbands of carvers as well.

Vera Feldman

Plastic Thumb Shield

I suffered many a bloody thumb when I started carving miniature ducks, and devised a shield to protect myself. I now use a thumb shield made from a section of plastic pipe, stuck on with sticking plaster. Any section of small diameter plastic pipe can be shaped to fit your thumb, and you could probably use masking tape instead of plasters.

John Clatworthy

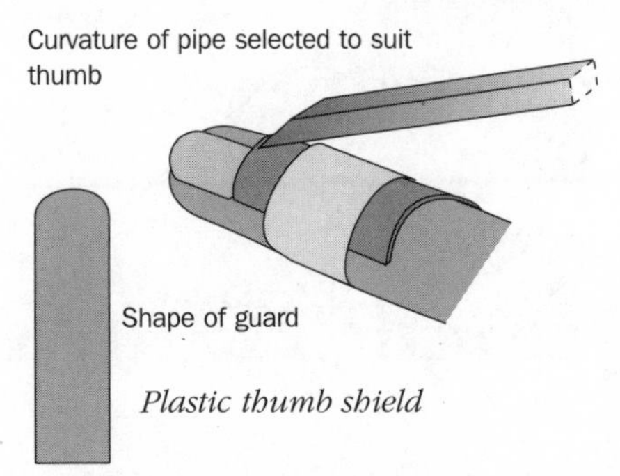

Plastic thumb shield

Less Noise

Woodcarving should be therapeutic, calming and peaceful, but the constant clack of a lignum vitae mallet against boxwood gouge handle can be irritating to yourself or neighbours. Using the palm of your hand may not be safe, comfortable or efficient.

I now use white rubber mallets made by Thor which not only reduce the noise level by at least half, but are also more comfortable to use. They cause less jarring of my joints and do not mark or damage tool handles, yet are dense enough to give a positive contact.

I have 10oz and 28oz mallets and these have superseded my beech and lignum ones.

Paul Goodrick

Chisels From Knives

I was pleased to discover I could cut down old, second-hand putty knives and scribing knives to make chisels. So far I have made two, both straight-edged. One blade is 28mm, 1⅛in, wide and the other 3mm, ⅛in, wide. They cost me £1 each.

I cut the excess blade off with a junior hacksaw and file down the shape, then file a bevel for the cutting edge. They both hold quite a keen edge and you don't need a grinder to get a good edge.

D.P. Thyer

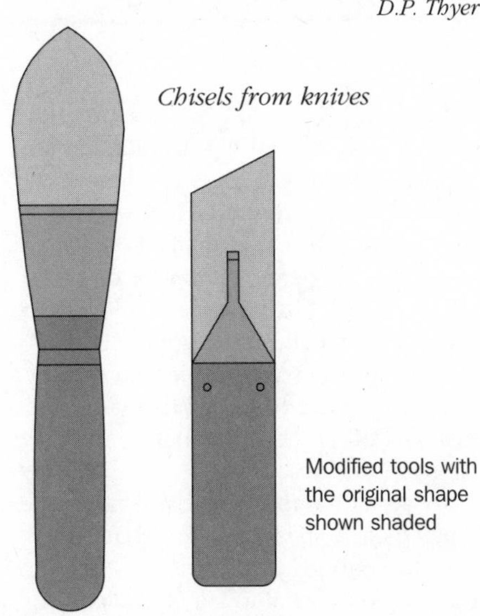

Chisels from knives

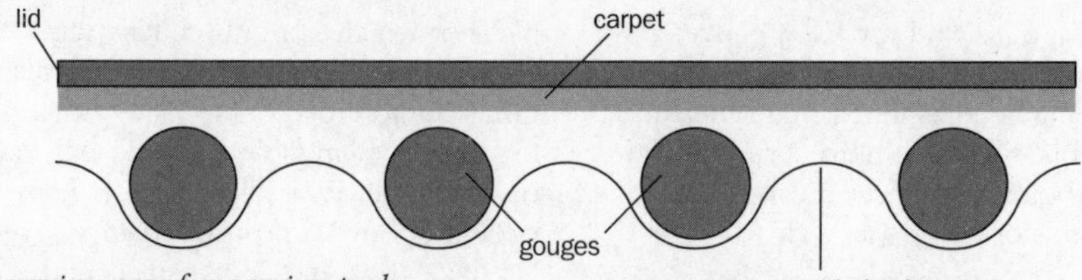

Carrying case for carving tools

Boxed Set

I needed to carry my carving tools to a sculpture class, and didn't want them rolling around loose in the carrying case/box.

I found that a piece of corrugated plastic roofing sheet with a small profile of about 35mm, 1⅜in, 'wavelength' took the gouges neatly. You could of course use larger profiles for bigger tools.

I stuck a piece of fabric to the plastic, not really necessary but it stops them rattling and adds a bit of elegance. Finally I lined the lid of the case/box with a carpet offcut, which holds the tools firmly in place.

Peter Warner

Switch Protection

Angle grinders fitted with cutting discs such as the Arbortech are efficient at rapid waste wood removal. However, they are so efficient at their job that sometimes the large amount of fine shavings and dust produced can clog up the on/off switch on the grinder.

This has happened to me on several occasions, and I have had to switch the machine off at the mains before de-clogging the switch.

To overcome this problem, I now tape a piece of plastic bag or fine material such as cotton over the switch. Put a fold in the material to allow movement without tearing, and if it is thin you can use it double.

Of course you must make sure the cooling vents in the grinder casing are not covered by the material or tape, or else it will overheat.

Rod Naylor

Switch protection

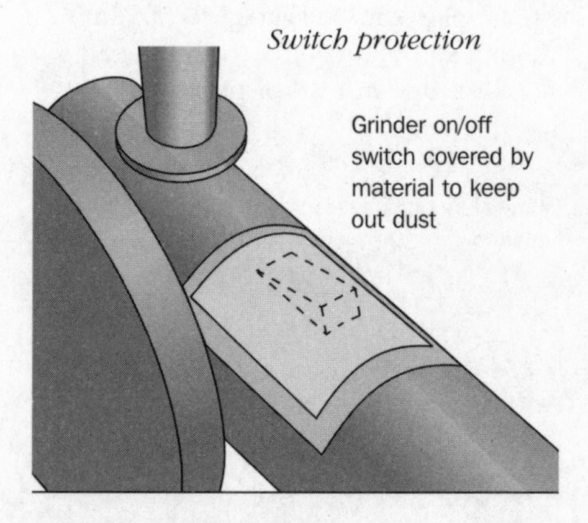

Fearsome Ferrules

I have damaged several fruit bowls and other deep carvings by forgetting to watch the whole of my gouge or chisel.

The problem is that I have concentrated so hard on carefully watching the cutting edge of the blade that I have forgotten to beware of the ferrule, which can cut lumps out of the bowl's edge.

Damage from ferrules can be reduced

by filing a radius on the sharp edge of the ferrule and also by placing a leather washer between the handle and the shoulder.

Rod Naylor

Rounder The Better

Native carvers in many Third World countries, particularly in the Far East, have to make their own tools, or get a metal blank from the local blacksmith which they sharpen themselves.

With a flat blank they make a flat gouge by grinding the end to as much arc as the blank will allow. Then, to increase the arc, they 'bullnose' the tool by grinding off the corners so the cutting edge is an arc. This in effect increases the sweep of the tool.

Some American carvers use the same trick to produce a firmer chisel that does not stick or leave lines on the wood at the edges of the cut. Even a little bullnosing will stop the catching.

E.J. Tangerman

Saw Point

Sawing wood and metal in tight corners can be difficult with conventional saws. Using a normal hacksaw is difficult because of the wing nut used to fix and tension the blade. And holding a hacksaw blade in your hand is neither safe nor comfortable.

I found the solution was to use a normal padsaw, but I filed the 10mm, ⅜in wide slotted throat in the handle out to 13mm, ½in, so it would take a standard hacksaw blade.

Because of the blade's flexibility it was not practical for it to extend more than 100mm, 4in from the handle, so I broke an old hacksaw blade in half by bending and then hammering it. (Be sure to wear hand, face and eye protection).

This gave me a suitable length of blade, with 50mm, 2in held in the handle by the saw's slotted screws. You do not normally use 50mm, 2in at each end of a hacksaw blade anyway because of the fixing points, so this gives a very useful tool with sharp teeth for no extra cost.

For cutting wood you can also use lengths of broken 10mm, ⅜in bandsaw blades, and of course you can still use the original padsaw blades.

Shaun Hoey

Bow-saw Blades

Bow-saw blades can be hard to find, and cost about £3 each, so I make my own – saving the cost and availability problems – by using lengths of bandsaw blade.

These are relatively cheap and enable me to have a range of width and grade blades to suit the job in hand. I find that 6mm, ¼in, x 6 tpi, ¼in x 10 tpi and 5mm, 3⁄16in, x 24 tpi handle just about any of the materials I am likely to use.

John Lakey

Padsaw fitted with hacksaw blade

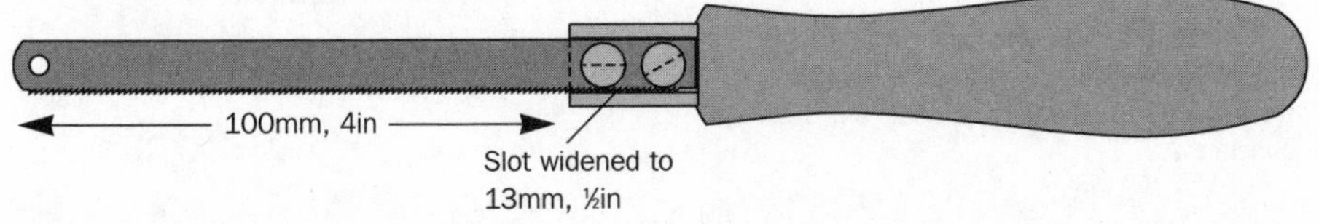

UNDERCUT IDEA

Deep undercuts are difficult to tackle with any traditional sanding tools. Rotary burrs are useful, but if they have to be used across the grain the fibres of the wood may be torn and show up as dark lines when polished.

One solution is to use a flexible drive machine with a reciprocating handpiece. Fine burrs, needle files and rifflers can be fitted rather than the usual chisel or gouge blades.

There are two problems. The first is these handpieces usually have a floating head so the gouges normally used will only cut when pressed into the wood.

To overcome this fit an elastic band through or around the head so it operates all the time, which is necessary for a sanding action.

The second problem is that burrs, rifflers or other tools may not have the correct diameter of handle or shank. Some burrs have interchangeable shanks, but others will require a bush or collet to enlarge the diameter of the tool.

This can be made by taking a small piece of metal tube, such as a broken radio aerial, and putting a cut or two down the side.

Rod Naylor

DEPTH GAUGE

The simplest and cheapest depth gauge for determining depth of setting-in on a relief carving is a nail or brad in a short stick. You simply drive in the brad until the head projects to the desired depth.

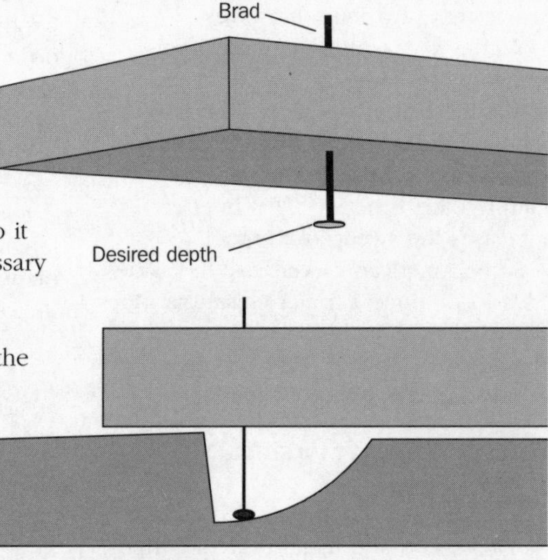

Moving the gauge over the relief

Depth Gauge

Undercut idea

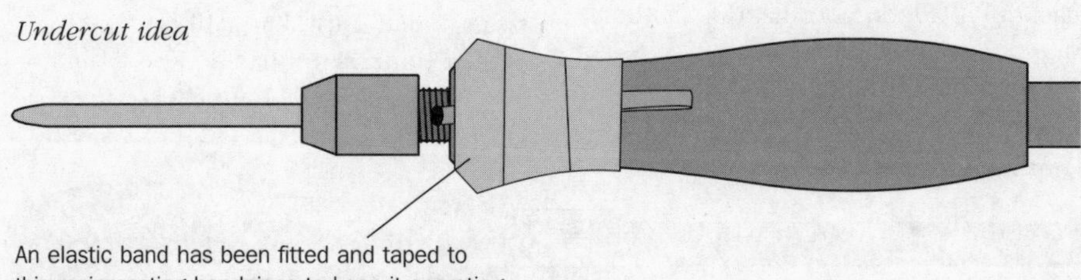

An elastic band has been fitted and taped to this reciprocating handpiece to keep it operating constantly

When you slide the stick over the set-in area it will wobble if the cut is not deep enough.

E.J. Tangerman

Rasps And Rifflers

Rasps and rifflers

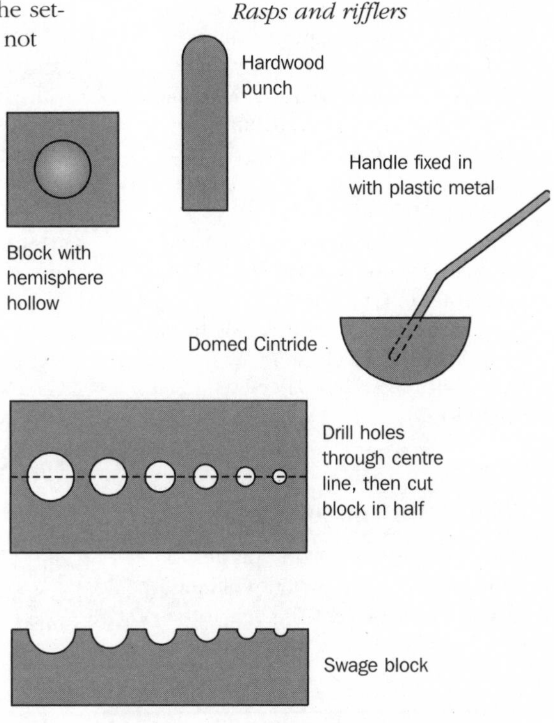

Sheets of sintered metal abrasive such as Cintride can be cut into cheap and handy rasps. However, achieving the double curves needed for rifflers is not so easy, and I have used techniques from my former career as a jeweller.

You need a jig like a silversmith's doming block and some punches, which you can make from a resilient hardwood like beech *(Fagus sylvatica)*. You will need two pieces about 75 x 75 x 25mm. 3 x 3 x 1in. Gouge out a hemispherical depression of 38mm, 1½in, diameter in one block and another of 25mm, 1in in the other.

You will also need a short length of hardwood dowel rounded at one end as a punch.

Cut the Cintride into the desired riffler shape, place it over the larger doming block, and with the dowel punch and a mallet tap lightly and evenly into the depression until it has reached the full depth.

If tighter curves are required transfer it to the smaller block and repeat the process. It doesn't seem necessary to anneal the Cintride for this amount of doming.

A useful shape for working on small hollows such as spoon bowls can be made using a 38mm, 1½in, circle of Cintride, doming it as described, and then filling the back with plastic metal. Insert a handle before it sets.

Half round and even round rasps can be made from Cintride by using a silversmith's swage block. Make your own from a block of beech 200 x 100 x 100mm, 8 x 4 x 4in.

Drill holes of the required size through the centre line of the block from about 25mm, 1in, down to 6mm, ¼in, then saw carefully along the centre line to make two swage blocks.

With the appropriate sized dowels it is then easy to form perfect half and full rounds.

Miniaturists may find it worthwhile buying a block. Brass doming blocks ➢

and steel punches are available with hemispheres from 32mm, 1¼in, downwards.

These can be expensive, but cheaper ones from India are available from: Manchester Minerals, Rooth Street, Heaton Norris, Stockport, Cheshire SK4 1DJ. Tel: 0161 477 0435.

Cintride strips in three grades and various sizes are available from DIY stores. A 183 x 90mm, 7¼ x 3½in strip costs around £3.70. Full details from: Cintride Ltd, Ashford Road Works, Bakewell, Derbyshire DE45 1GL. Tel: 01629 812513.

Ruth Harvey

Fingerstall Thumb Shield

Many people use sticking plaster to protect their thumb when whittling or carving small pieces. This has to be put on and off each time which is messy and time consuming.

I have made a thumb shield which can be put on and off quickly and easily without the need for messy adhesive.

You will need a leather or plastic fingerstall used to secure dressings. This can be bought from a chemist. You will also need a small piece of flexible metal sheet, the type covered on one side with imitation leather, which can be bought from craft shops.

Cut and bend the metal sheet to the size and shape to fit round your thumb. File and smooth the edges, coat the metal side with adhesive, and insert it into the fingerstall.

The lower edge of the insert can be covered with plastic insulation tape which is pulled over and stuck to the outside of the fingerstall to make a comfortable and permanent thumb shield.

C.D. Atkinson

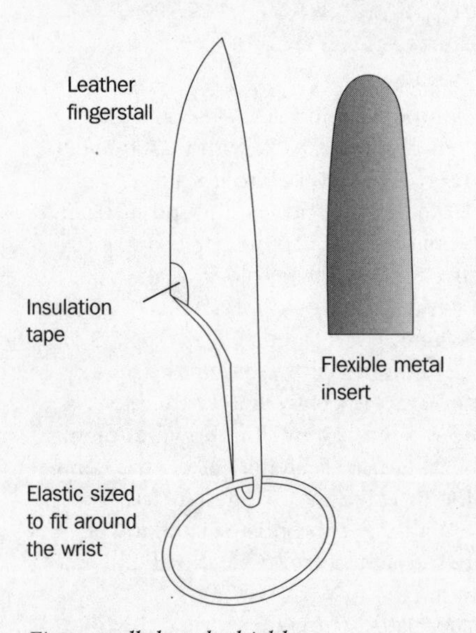

Fingerstall thumb shield

Hand Mallet

I found the shape of standard carving mallets awkward and uncomfortable, so I made my own mallet block to fit the shape of my hand. It is about 170 x 75 x 70mm, 6¾ x 3 x 2¾in.

The most suitable wood to hand at the time was a piece of jarrah *(Eucalyptus marginata)*, and this has served me well for 30 years, but a piece of boxwood *(Buxus sempervirens)* or lignum vitae *(Guaiacum officinale)* would have been better.

The shape is really comfortable so you can use it for longer without fatigue.

C.E. Fisher

(See illustration on next page)

The hand block mallet

170mm, 6¾in
75mm, 3in
Elevation
Plan
70mm, 2¾in

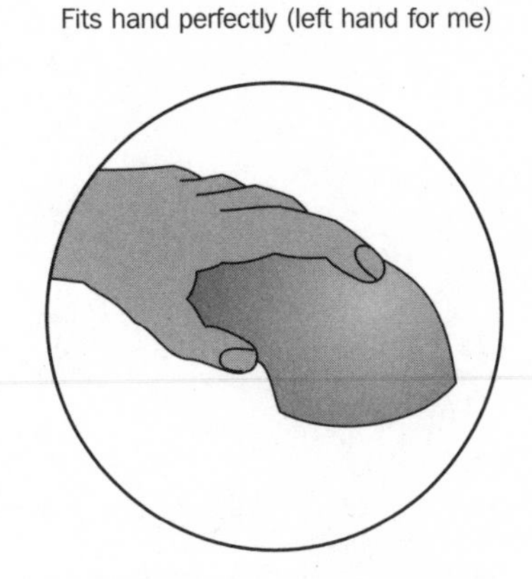

Key Tool

I have recently taken up carving and have concentrated on small wildlife subjects carved from 75mm, 3in square section wood. This means the eyes of the subjects have been small, and I found it difficult to get neatly cut eye pupils.

To overcome this, I found old pipe keys could be adapted to make small circular cutters. Friends of mine gave me lots of old keys with inner diameters ranging from about 3mm, ⅛in to 8mm, 5/16in.

I cut the key lug off with a hacksaw and smooth the cut surface with a file. I file down the outer diameter of the key barrel to produce a sharp edge, and put a small taper on the inner diameter using the end of a suitable size file tang as the cutting tool.

The key handle gives a good grip so the key can be turned in a rotary fashion to cut a clean circle for the eye pupil irrespective of the direction of the grain of the wood.

T.G. Laidler

Key tool

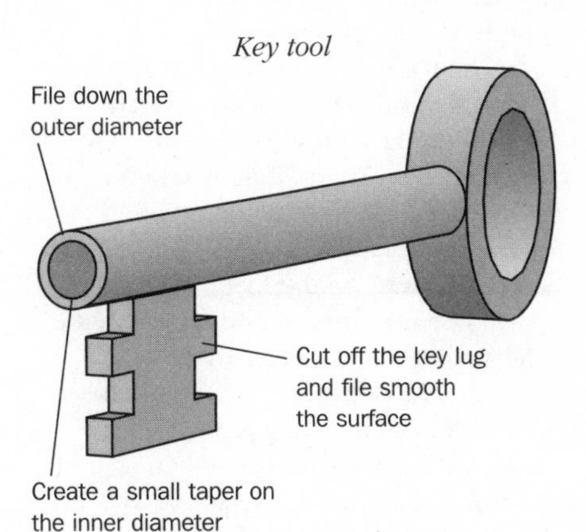

Shave Hook Scraper

Scrapers are a pleasure to use, but can be a real pain to sharpen, even straight ones. I have had no problems sharpening plane or spokeshave blades, though, so for this reason I have switched to using cheap shave hooks for scraping.

I use the 305mm, 12in long handled ones with changeable blades. More ➢

Shave hook and blades

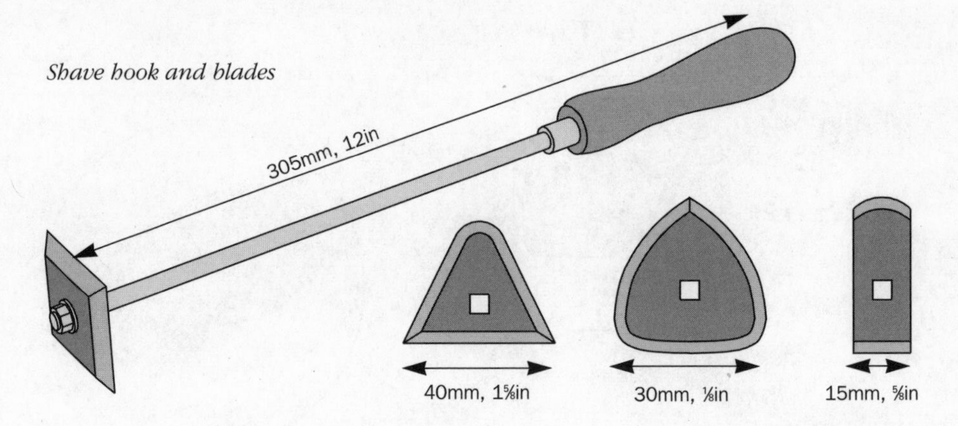

expensive fixed blade shave hooks are impossible to sharpen properly in a home workshop.

My shave hook came with a set of four different shaped blades which could be reground to other shapes if required. You sharpen them as you would a spokeshave blade.

The long handle enables you to apply good pressure on the blade without burning your thumbs, and although the blades are much smaller than conventional scrapers, I do not believe the width of cut is any less.

Another advantage is you can scrape right into recessed corners, and you can use them with one hand, which can be useful for work which is difficult to clamp.

My only reservation is that while the quality of the steel was adequate for a tool costing just £2, the grinding of the bevel and face was poor and required some major resharpening.

Readers could well find this tool a good alternative to an expensive scorp.

Frank Norman

Awkward Corners

Sanding in awkward corners is often possible with emery boards, available from any chemist. They are available in various grits, sizes and degrees of flexibility.

Another small shaping tool I find very useful for getting smooth flowing lines in leaf veins or drapery is a broken abrafile blade which can be used like a fine riffler.

You can make a handle by pushing one end into a piece of wood or a bottle cork.

Corks are also useful as sanding blocks as they can easily be shaped into the desired curvature.

Rod Naylor

Colour Coded Handles

For storing and carrying my carving tools around I use an old LP record case with a flap lid and gusset front panel. Inside is fitted an H-shaped stand with holes drilled in the cross piece to hold the gouges. This holds 28 tools.

With this arrangement you can see

only the ends of the handles, so I developed a colour coding system using a small dot of paint or permanent felt tip pen on the tops of the handles.

I use the snooker colour points system for the sweeps, thus red is 1, yellow 2, green 3, brown 4, blue 5, pink 6 and black 7. I extended this with white for 8 and grey for 9.

The smallest gouge of any sweep has a small dot of the appropriate colour, and larger gouges of that sweep have dots getting progressively larger.

Tools with a two digit number sweep have two dabs of paint, thus a No 11 has two spots of red, and a No 47 grounding tool a spot of brown and one of black.

I drill a small hollow in the handle top before applying the paint as this gives tidy circles.

Of course this colour coding system is equally effective for tools stored in a rack or in a tool roll.

F.J. Biggs

Bendy Blades

As a pensioner with many years of amateur carving, here is a tip I have found essential for my carving in the round.

Old, worn or broken hacksaw blades can make excellent tools. Being tempered only on the toothed side, they make really handy rifflers which will bend to pass through a gap or shape a feature. They will continue to cut wood when too worn for metal.

They can be held at both ends if bound with tape, or the back can be sharpened to make a cabinet scraper.

Snapped blades can have their ends ground to shape for fiddly things which would need special chisels. I still have rifflers, but use them only rarely.

Arthur Holland

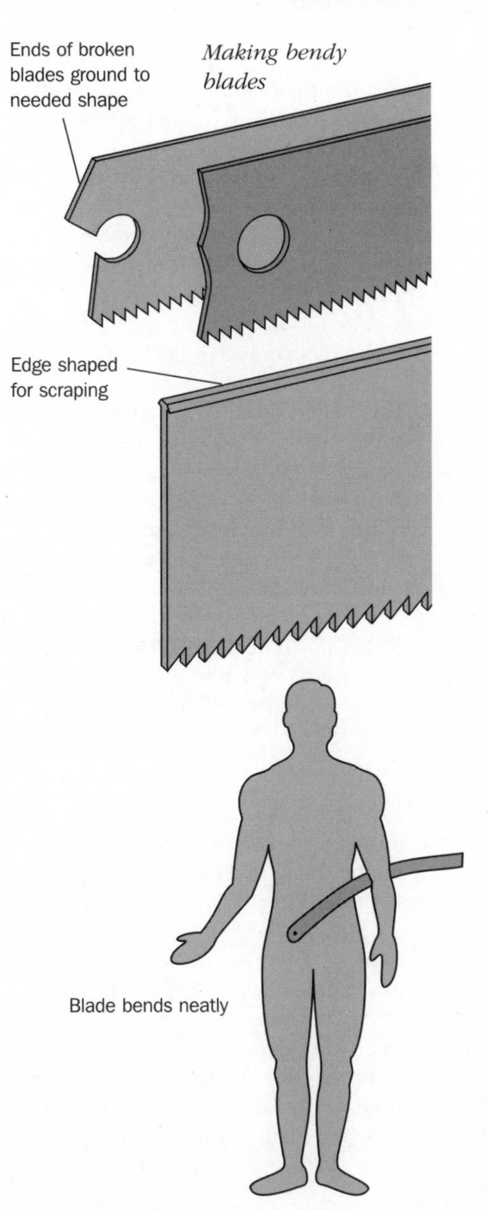

Making bendy blades

Mini Gouges

Aspiring woodcarvers, or those taking up any woodwork, have to be concerned about cost. Tools, equipment and wood are now all quite expensive, so readers may be interested in a low cost source of small carving tools.

Needle files and even masonry nails can be easily ground and shaped into straight or skew chisels, but it is more difficult to find materials for gouges.

An answer is to use an old umbrella. The spines have a deep U profile and can be found in different sizes. They can be cut to convenient lengths, and ground and honed to an edge.

The lengths are then glued into suitable pieces of wood which are shaped as required for handles.

Those with more expertise or ambition can heat treat the metal and shape it to produce a wide variety of small tools of all sorts of shapes and sizes.

I have used such tools with great success on boxwood *(Buxus sempervirens)* and have found no problem keeping a sharp cutting edge.

Peter Benson

Leather Guards

I wanted to protect my carving tools while travelling to evening classes, but didn't want to carry a bulky tool roll as I had only a few tools.

I bought a suede skirt for 10p at a jumble sale and made individual protective sheaths for all my tools.

First I cut down the seam to open up the skirt to one continuous length. Then I laid each tool on the suede with the handle just clear and marked out oblongs, allowing 12mm, ½in each side for joining, and 12mm, ½in at the end where the suede folded over, so the tool would not cut through the finished sheath.

After cutting out the suede it is doubled, or folded over and can be sewn, stapled or glued to make the sheath.

Mine were sewn. With leather it is best to puncture holes through first with a spike such as a nail, and use a good strong needle and nylon/polyester thread.

Most of my sheaths are still in use after 10 years' use and have undoubtedly saved wear and tear on my tools.

With the remaining suede I made a leather apron by attaching a length of strong linen tape to what remained of the skirt's waistband.

Patricia Vardigans

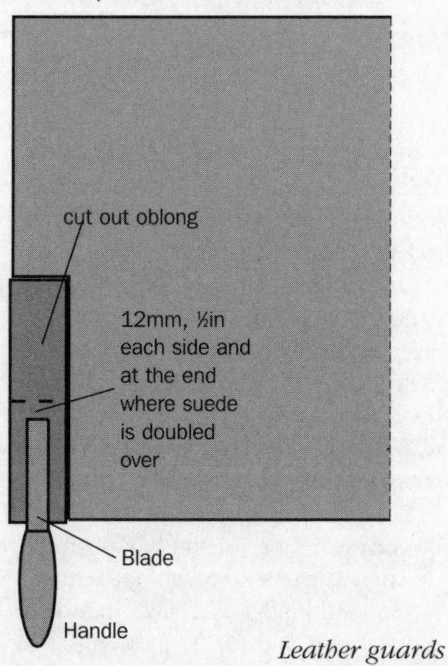

Leather guards

Profile Gauge

Last Christmas a friend gave me one of those nail sculpture devices that were in all the gimmick gift shops. It had hundreds of shiny nails set in a clear plastic covered block. These took the shape of anything pressed into them.

The novelty soon wore off and the device was consigned to a drawer.

However, I was recently looking for a way to show the curvature of the forehead to a student who was carving a head, and dug out the nails gadget.

By carefully manipulating the nails on our faces we ended up with a very clean profile that solved the problem.

Since then the device has proved invaluable as an aid to understanding the forms of a variety of objects and body parts such as mouths, noses and hands that often cause problems to student carvers.

For some reason it seems easier to appreciate the form when shown like this than when seen as part of the whole. I guess this is something to do with what we see as opposed to what we think we know.

Peter Benson

Editor's note: It may also have something to do with the uniform colour of the shape in a nail sculpture like this. Many beginners confuse changes in colour with the changes in light and shade due to the shape. Black and white photographs can also be useful in reducing this confusion.

Finger Guards

Doing a lot of detailed sanding can make your fingertips sore. I found the answer was to use baseball batters' or golfers' gloves. These are made of very thin leather and are well vented.

You can increase the life of the gloves by sticking two layers of masking tape over the ends of your thumb and first two fingers. This prevents your nails from cutting the thin leather but does not add too much bulk to interfere with the feel of the work.

Raymond Stovich

SECTION 2
SHARPENING

SHARPENING V-TOOLS

Sharpening a v-tool (also known as a parting tool or cut-off tool) seems to involve tricks that even some expert carvers don't know or use.

First the cutting edges should be at right-angles to the line of the shank of the tool – not rounded or angled back or forward.

Second, if you look straight on at the cutting edges you will see that the metal is clearly thicker at the apex of the vee. Even careful sharpening will leave either a small blunt spot or a hook. And here is my tip, remove this blunt area by slightly – very slightly – flattening the bottom of the vee. Then hone lightly inside the bottom of the vee with a suitably shaped slip stone, stroking outwards only.

This technique can also be used in sharpening other tools with corners in the cross-section, such as the macaroni.

E.J. Tangerman

POLISH FLUTES

Many people are now honing their tools with honing machines, which use felt or paper wheels dressed with an abrasive paste. One of the advantages with these honing machines is that they don't form a burr, so a slip stone is not required to remove it before carving.

However, I have discovered that a tool can be razor sharp from a honing machine, but still not cut well. This is due to minute rust spots on the inside of the flute that would have been removed by the slip stone when backing off.

The solution is to occasionally buff inside the flute near the cutting edge, so that both sides of the blade are polished.

Rod Naylor

Section 3
TECHNIQUES

Letter Ideas

One of the main difficulties with letter carving is the initial design of the work.

There are two aspects to this, the design of the individual letters and their spacing into words and phrases.

Carvers have traditionally used books containing alphabets of letters in different typefaces. Individual letters can be selected, scaled and arranged to spell the desired words.

However, this is not a straightforward process and mistakes at this stage can easily ruin a carving before it is really begun.

I use a word processor package running on a standard personal computer. This contains 32 different typefaces, each in 15 different sizes.

I can easily write the type and size I want and print it out full size for copying directly on to the wood.

This method is not only faster than doing it manually but removes a number of potential errors such as incorrect spacing or alignment.

Suitable computer systems cost around £1,000, but you may have a friend with one, and they are often available in schools, colleges and libraries.

David Eustace.

Lettering Layout

When initially laying out an inscription for carving I find it best to roughly draw the letters using chalk – to assess their placement and spacing.

Chalk can easily be removed with a damp cloth, and letters, words and spacing can be simply adjusted so that the inscription is visually pleasing, and correct when viewed from a distance.

When the layout is correct it can be redrawn more accurately using a pencil.

Zoë Gertner

Hollow Hint

Large carvings can split over a period of time, especially if the wood is not fully seasoned, or placed in changing conditions of temperature and humidity.

One way of avoiding this is to hollow out the unseen surface, if the carving has a flat back or base. The hollowing allows the wood to move and considerably reduces the chance of splitting.

Rod Naylor

Tracing Film

When carving in relief one problem is that any carving removes details drawn on the face of the wood. The carver then has the problem of reinstating the drawn detail at each level of the carving. Usually this is done by producing a duplicate drawing on tracing paper and flipping this backwards and forwards each time detail needs to be redrawn.

The problem for someone like me, ➢

who takes a long time to finish a carving, is that tracing paper not only becomes increasingly opaque with age but it also shrinks.

I have overcome this by using acetate film, used by graphic artists and for overhead projectors. As it is transparent it gives a crystal clear view of the carving through the film. Acetate film is much more flexible and durable than tracing paper, though it is a little more expensive.

Film and the pens to draw on it are available from good stationers and art supplies shops.

Peter Benson

Tracing Figures

I am quite new to carving and have found great enjoyment from copying sculptures that can be obtained from a number of sources. The difficulty is to transfer a silhouette on to a block prior to bandsawing.

I came up with the idea of this simply made instrument to overcome the problem and thought that it might help other readers.

To trace an outline, stand or lay the sculpture on drawing paper on a flat surface. Follow the outline of the sculpture with the plastic insert while exerting gentle pressure on the pencil. The outline can then be transferred to the block – I usually cut round the outline with scissors then I can draw round this on to the block.

You then repeat the process with the other elevations of the sculpture to get an all round picture.

Ted Jeffery

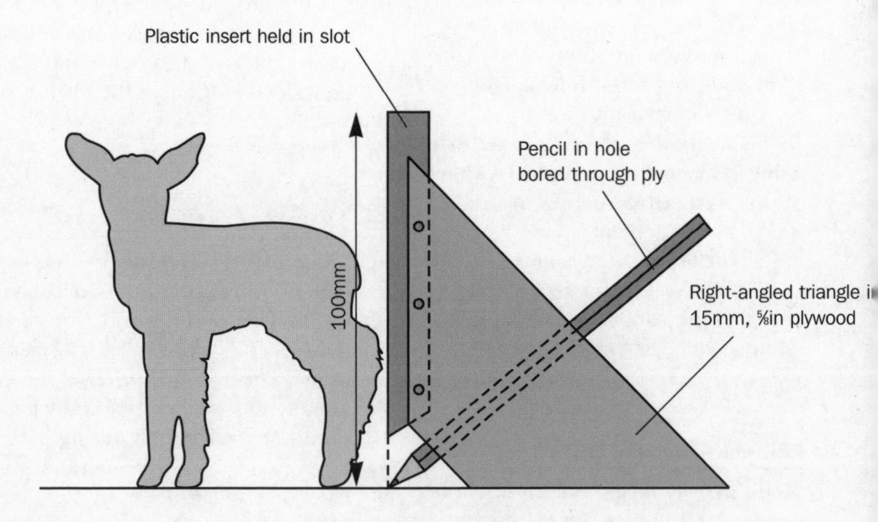

Tracing figures

Faster Cut

You can easily modify carving copying machines to greatly increase their cutting speed by exchanging the normal router for an angle grinder fitted with a cutting disc such as an Arbortech.

Depending on the type of disc used, this can increase the number of cuts by up to 100,000 per minute.

You then replace the router for adding fine detail.

Rod Naylor

Card Cutout

As a late newcomer to carving and whittling, I like to outline a design on the wood before starting work.

First I draw the design on paper, then I transfer this to stiff card, either with carbon paper or by blacking the back of the drawing paper with soft pencil. It is best to stick the paper to the card with sticky tape to prevent it slipping while doing this.

I then cut out the card, including any cutouts in the design, and use the card as a template to draw the design on to the wood. The advantage of the card is it can be kept as a template for when the drawn design disappears from the wood as it is cut back in carving.

John Jones

Repeat Panels

When making panels of fretwork, blind frets and similar low reliefs, I use a copy carving machine rather than a fretsaw.

I first use the fretsaw to make a template. Only one pattern repeat is required. I stick this on to the copier with double sided sticky tape and use the machine to repeatedly copy from this fragment to create the required length.

Using this method I have achieved time savings of over 90% compared to traditional hand methods. I still use this system even for one-offs, as a library of templates can be stored for future use.

Rod Naylor

Bench Height

Most workbenches designed for general woodwork are too low for carving. This can result in you working almost bent double like a letter C and finding it difficult to straighten up after a long session.

For carving, your bench top should be from 38in, 965mm to 41in, 1041mm high, depending on your height, much higher than the average table or workbench.

My bench was made by a carpenter following instructions in Eleanor Rowe's book *Practical Woodcarving*, first published by Batsford around 1918. She was manager of the School of Art Woodcarving, South Kensington for 20 years, and I found her book invaluable during my final year at the City and Guilds Art School.

I would also suggest using one of those office swivel chairs with infinitely adjustable height so you can sit at your bench when relevant.

Mary Anstee-Parry

Cheap Shaping

Rifflers are expensive and may not be available in the shape you want. A cheap alternative is to use a piece of flexible abrasive and bend it round a piece of dowel or shaped block. You ➢

can use glue or double-sided adhesive tape to hold it in place.

The most efficient abrasive is tungsten carbide flexible sheet such as Grit-Cote which is almost everlasting when used on wood and so works out much cheaper than glasspaper in the long run.

Also, unlike traditional rifflers, these home-made sticks cut on both forward and backward strokes.

Rod Naylor

Extra Bench

I have a good workbench which is fine for general woodwork and carpentry, but too low for carving. To remedy this I made a small extra bench which I hold on top of the bench in the vice and further secure with a bench holdfast or G cramp. You could also use it on a Workmate.

The bench is made from scrap wood and I can nail or screw work to it without damaging the main bench. Mine measures 760 x 255mm, 30 x 10in and it stands on 50mm, 2in runners, but you can make them of the right size to make it the height you want. Make sure all screws are well countersunk

Stan Herbert

Glue Guide

I often do small, delicate carvings which have to be fixed on to another piece of wood to be held while carving.

I do this with hot melt glue, direct on to the wood rather than using the conventional glue and brown paper in between method. This means it is ready in minutes rather than hours.

When I have finished the carving I put it in the microwave oven for between 15 and 50 seconds depending on the size. This melts the glue and then the pieces can easily be parted by hand without any force.

H.T. Bolliger

Carving bench

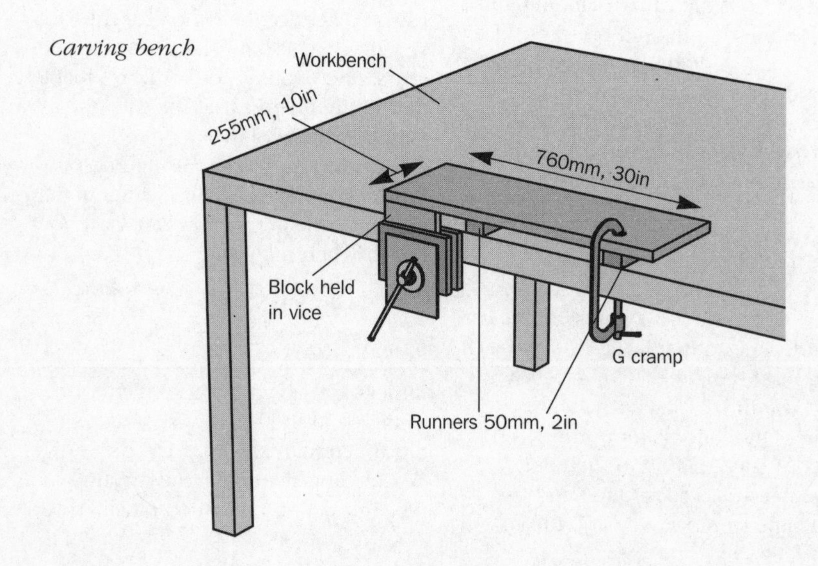

Hot-melt Glue

I note there has been some discussion about the merits of hot-melt glue for temporary workholding. I use it frequently for carving and turning and it is quite adequate if you follow some simple guidelines.

First, you cannot use it direct on cold metal (e.g. carving clamp or faceplate) as the metal cools the glue before it can spread and flow properly over the surface. The metal needs to be heated to about 100-120°C with a blowtorch, not enough to affect temper or cause distortion.

Glue should also be applied to the wood and the blowtorch played briefly across that as well to re-melt it, taking care not to scorch the wood. Bring the surfaces together with hot melted glue on both.

You must wait a few minutes for the glue to cool before attempting to work on the wood. The carving can be easily removed and repositioned later by heating the metal again.

Cleaning up the base of the wood afterwards can be difficult for carvers. (Turners should design the work so it can be cut off with a parting tool.) The best tip I have is to use an iron set to the cool end of the cotton range (no steam) and some kitchen towel or newspaper. Iron the paper on and the glue will stick to the paper, but be quick to remove the iron before the glue soaks right through on to it.

Peel the paper off while the glue is still hot and runny and repeat as necessary. I find four or five pieces is usually enough, depending on how smooth the base was when you started. This will not leave the base ready for polishing, but you can clean the rest off with a cabinet scraper, or cover it with green baize.

A final tip: a layer of sanding sealer applied before the glue can make it easier to clean off, with little loss of adhesion.

Of course normal safety precautions should be taken when using a naked flame in the workshop. There should be no loose wood shavings or dust around, and all flammable materials such as sanding sealer must be covered and sealed.

Allan Denton

Sanding Jig For Thin Leaves

I like to carve natural scenes, or habitat, and it is difficult getting the pieces thin enough. I didn't want to use metal as I wanted to be a woodworker, not a metalworker.

I developed my own sanding jig for working down wood into thin sheets which are suitable for making leaves, flowers or other thin, delicate pieces. I find tupelo *(Nyssa aquatica)* is the best wood for this kind of work.

I use a hand-held sanding machine, held horizontally in a vice, and a 50 x 12mm, 2 x ½in sanding drum. This is used over a tapered block. The thickness of the wood sheet is gauged by the distance of the tapered wood block from the sanding drum.

The wood block is a 305mm, 12in, long section cut from an old 100 x 100mm, 4 x 4in fence post. On top of this is glued a piece of wood 305mm, 12in long x 100mm, 4in wide and tapered from 25mm, 1in thick to nothing.

The block has 60 grit abrasive paper glued to the bottom to keep it from ➢

Sanding drum thicknesser

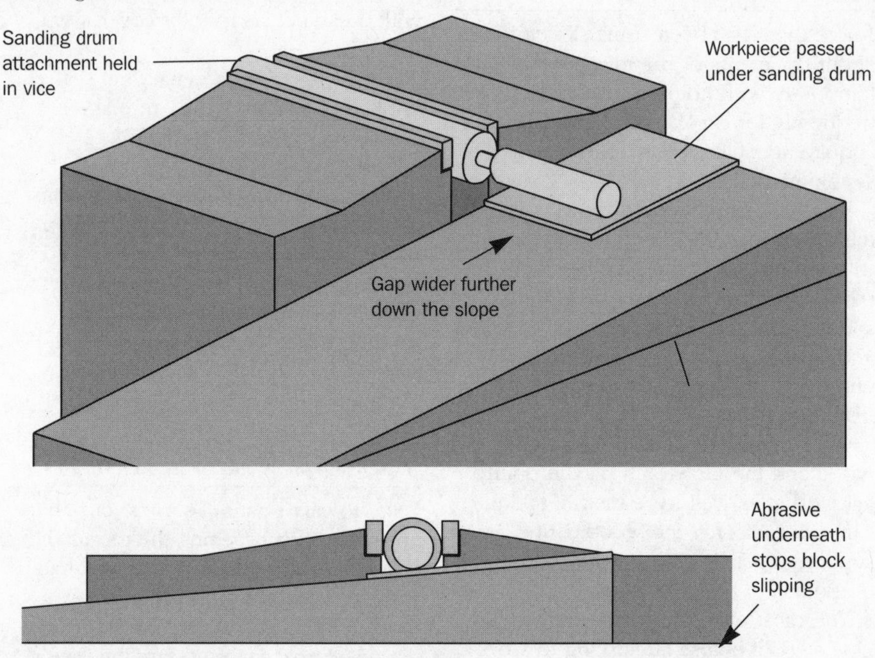

slipping on the bench.

I cut out a piece of wood slightly larger than I need, and feed it through my miniature planer/thicknesser. I gradually move the block along, sanding down the wood in small increments until it is the thickness I want. I have got some pieces down to one hundredth of an inch.

James Baxter

Banish Zits

On one of my earlier carvings, I sanded the surface meticulously and then polished it. Several months later there was a prolonged period of rain and each pore in the wood erupted like a miniature volcano, ruining the piece.

Now when I sand, I finish with the finest grade of paper, and then thoroughly wet the wood. This makes all the wood that has been compressed into the pores swell up. When it is dry I re-sand. This prevents another outbreak of zits.

Rod Naylor

Cover-up

Small scratches on white painted wood are irritating, but they can be easily hidden by using white shoe polish.

Debbie Wilcox

A Light Touch

On hardwoods, particularly large sculptures, there is some need to reach areas with long-bent or short-bent gouges. These must be used with some caution, because they tend to spring if driven with a heavy mallet – causing stepped irregularities in the cut. The answer is to use a smaller mallet and lighter blows. Or, you could take a little longer to do the shaping by hand.

These are not problems in ordinary panel carving, so do not justify the addition of bent tools to the basic straight ones, unless you really need them. Many carvers think that more tools means better carving – golfers find to their sorrow that more clubs are not the answer.

E.J. Tangerman

Avoid Breakage

A major cause of tool breakage, particularly in tough woods like ash, is the tendency of a driven tool to stick in the cut. It is not the fault of the wood or the tool, the problem lies with the carver.

In most cases the tool has been driven in too deeply, then the carver becomes impatient and tries to wedge, pry or twist the tool to get it loose. It's no wonder that the tools break; thin tools, like v-tools and small chisels, are hard tempered steel and are not pry bars.

If a tool won't roll out of the cut sideways, a chip must be cut cleanly on all edges so that the tool can be removed without levering. Cut away wood around the tool's stuck edge and pull it back out in the direction it was jammed in.

E.J. Tangerman

Push And Pull Cuts

I have a student who uses a coping saw to do much of the shaping of the animal or human figures he carves in basswood *(Tilia americana)*, saving himself hours of whittling to reach the desired shape.

We argue about whether the saw blade should be fitted to the scroll or coping saw to give a push or pull cut.

I favour the Japanese idea of mounting the blade so it cuts on the pull stroke. I believe this works best on hard woods where cutting on the push stroke can be inaccurate and likely to cause blade breakage in tight turns. Try the pull stroke cut, you may be surprised at how well it works.

I think my student may be right to prefer the push cut on soft woods, but on hard woods I can draw cut much faster and more accurately.

There is a possibility that the pull cut will cause some slight splitting on the front side of the workpiece rather than on the back, but those surfaces will be cut away anyway when modelling the piece.

If you are doing pierce cutting the pull stroke is far superior to the push stroke and you model away the burrs and slight edge breakage.

E.J. Tangerman

SECTION 4
CLAMPS AND WORKHOLDERS

MODIFIED WORKHOLDER

I have been using this addition to my workholder for some time now and find it very useful. It uses two sets of sash-cramp heads (the sort you can buy to make your own sash-cramps with), some 50 x 25mm, 2 x 1in, timber and a base board.

The size of the base board and the length of the rails can be made to suit different sizes of carving or relief panel. I have two different sizes made up and just swap the cramp heads over.

J.R. Benham

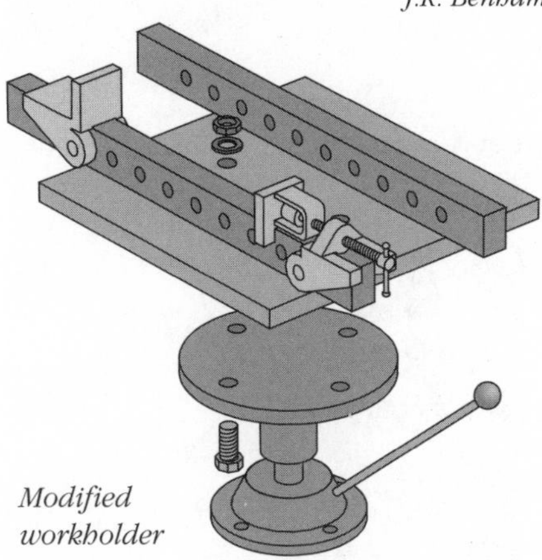

Modified workholder

TOUGH WORKHOLDER

I wanted a sturdy workholder capable of holding large carving blocks.

I got my local blacksmith to cut two squares of 12mm, ½in steel plate, one 150mm, 6in square, the other 75mm, 3in square.

Four holes were drilled near the corners of each square, and a 150mm, 6in length of scaffolding pole was welded to the centre of each plate.

I fixed the larger of the base plates to the side panel of my heavy carving bench with coach screws. The smaller plate, which holds the workpiece, is fixed to the other with a scaffolding clip, the type which bolts two tubes together at right angles.

The result is a very strong workholder which can be rotated in both horizontal and vertical planes through 360°. It holds large items with no movement in any position, even upside down.

Frank Biggs

Tough workholder

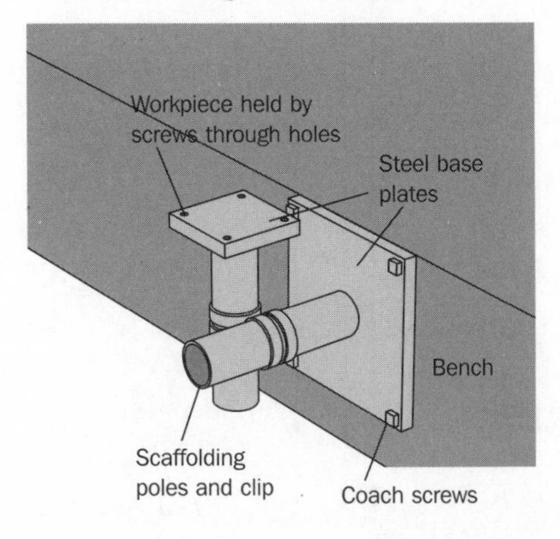

Painting Project

I often carve small birds, sometimes six at a time, and holding them for painting was a problem until I came up with this idea.

I got six 125mm, 5in lengths of 8mm dowelling and drilled a 6mm, ¼in diameter hole about 6mm, ¼in deep into the end of each.

Next I fitted the head of a 15mm, ⅝in long brass screw into each hole with two-part putty. You could also use wood filler or epoxy resin.

The screw is fixed to the body of each bird. I use jelutong *(Dyera costulata)* and the grain is soft enough for the small screw hole to be pushed closed afterwards.

Each dowel is put into a turntable which is 255mm, 10in diameter and has 9mm holes drilled through 20mm, ¾in in from the edge. These hold the dowels so I can paint all six birds at once.

Bob Richardson

On the Mat

You can hold work more securely on the bench for carving without it slipping, and prevent it being marked, by covering the top of the bench with a piece of high density foam.

Suitable materials include sleeping mats from camping shops or wet suit rubber from sports shops.

Rod Naylor

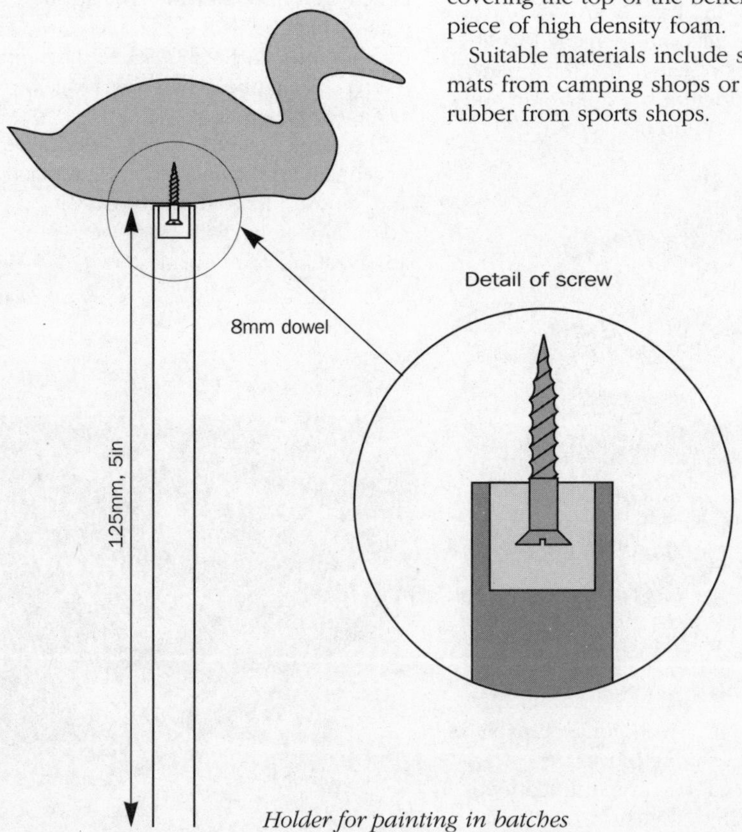

Holder for painting in batches

TOE-HOLD

Like many songbird carvers I enjoy the challenge and satisfaction of making my own bird feet, rather than buying moulded, pre-cast ones.

One of the most difficult processes is holding all the toes in place on the tarsus at once while soldering them, without them moving.

I have tried most of the suggested methods, such as taping, stapling,

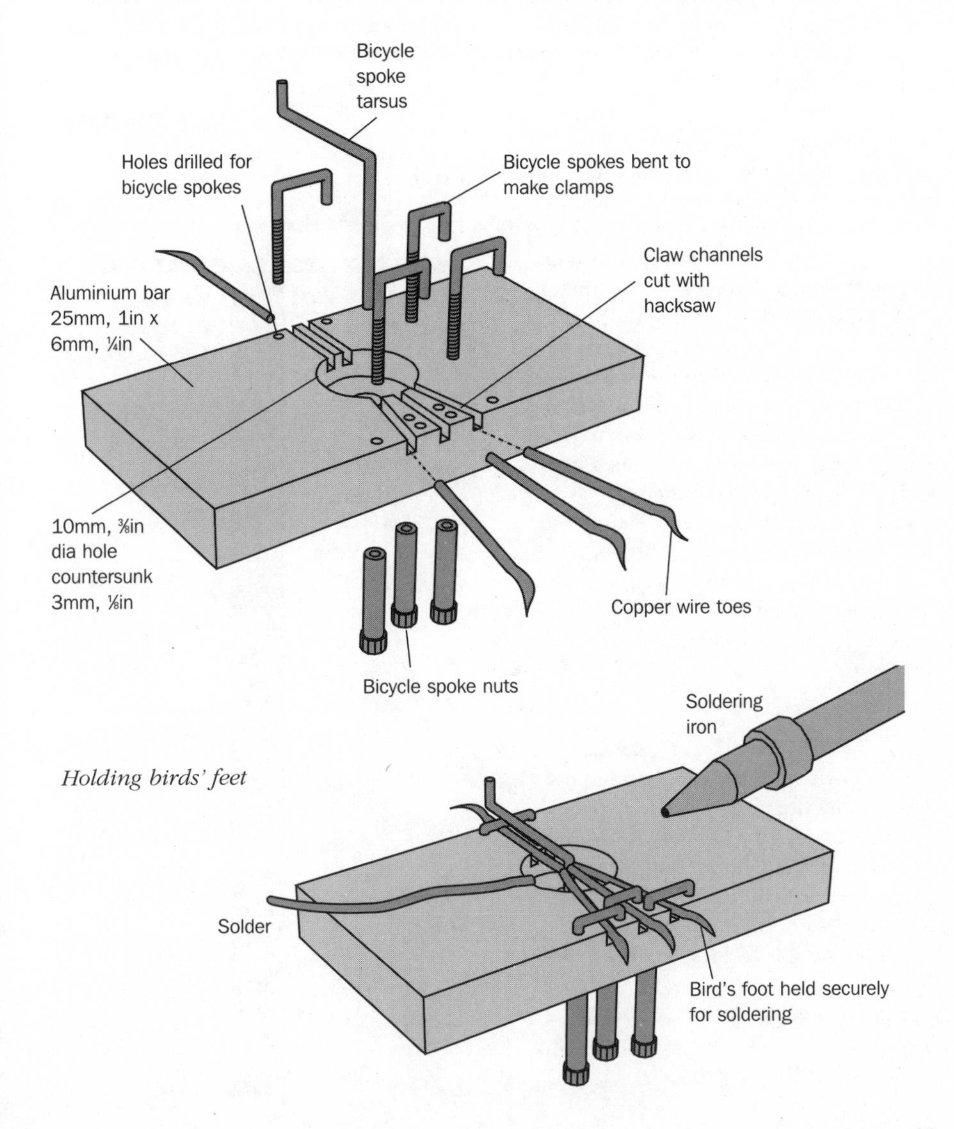

Holding birds' feet

alligator clips and twisting wires together, but have found none of them entirely satisfactory.

Now I have developed a jig to hold all the parts firmly without moving while I solder.

I use bicycle spokes for my tarsus, and hit upon this idea when looking at the threaded spoke ends and tightening nuts I had clipped off the spokes.

Using a piece of 25 x 6mm, 1 x ¼in aluminium bar for the jig base, I cut grooves for the toes and drilled holes to hold the hooks made from spokes.

The toes are clamped firmly in place in the grooves by the spokes and nuts.

I countersank a 10mm, ⅜in diameter hole 3mm, ⅛in deep where all the parts come together to prevent the aluminium drawing heat away from the solder joint.

This jig can be used for most types and sizes of songbird. It is easy to make with a few simple tools such as a vice, drill and hacksaw. Note there are two grooves for the back toe to enable the making of both left and right feet.

It is best to cut the grooves so they are angled upwards towards the centre as this allows for a more natural setting of the toes on the tarsus.

Jim Dupont

TOUGH GALLOWS

I have made a hefty gallows stand for holding my decoy and figure carvings.

This consists of a 400mm, 16in length of 25mm, 1in square x 6mm, ¼in thick steel tube, drilled through on all four sides to lighten it. On to one end is welded a length of 25 x 6mm, 1 x ¼in flat steel.

The flat steel is drilled through to take wood screws which are driven into the underside of the carving.

The gallows stand is held in a standard metal bench vice and can be tilted anywhere along the left/right axis. By releasing the vice and turning the stand to the next face you turn the carving through 90°.

I have two stands, one with a flat of 100mm, 4in long for small carvings, and the other with a flat 180mm, 7in long for full-size birds.

Brad Parkes

Gallows stand

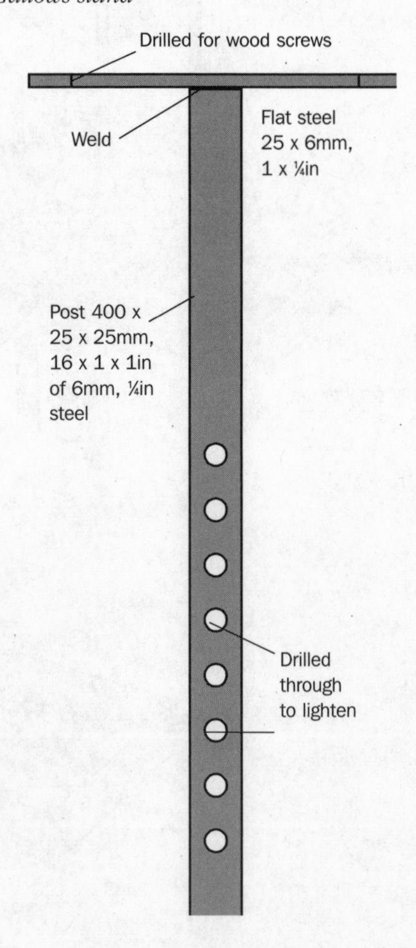

Dogged Idea

Here's an idea for holding difficult shapes if you don't have the appropriate bench dogs.

Dowels

Bench vice

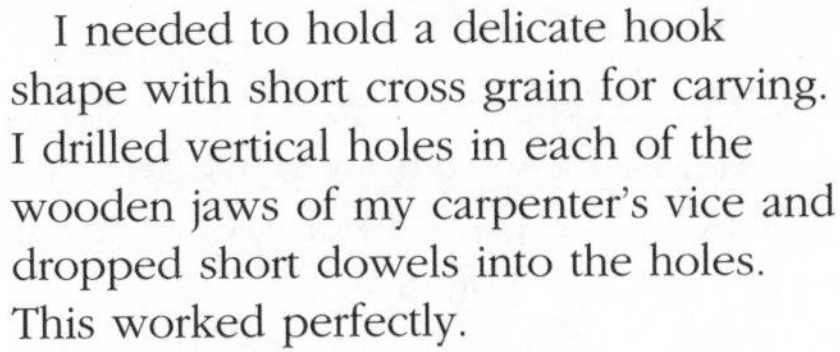

I needed to hold a delicate hook shape with short cross grain for carving. I drilled vertical holes in each of the wooden jaws of my carpenter's vice and dropped short dowels into the holes. This worked perfectly.

For really awkward shapes you could make up custom jaws from MDF with holes to drop over the dowels. Three holes and dowels could be used for a three-point clamp.

T.J. Austen

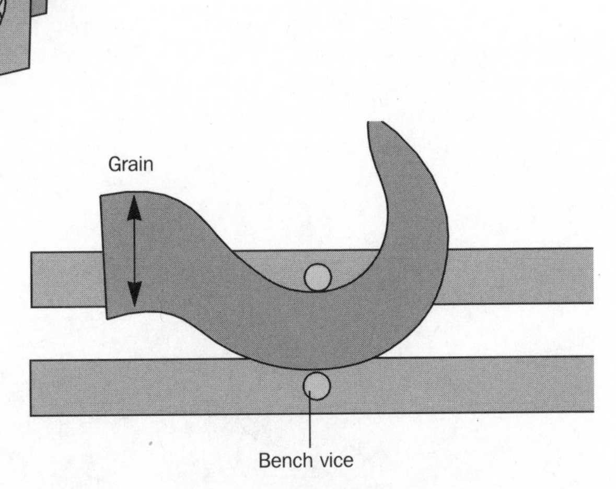

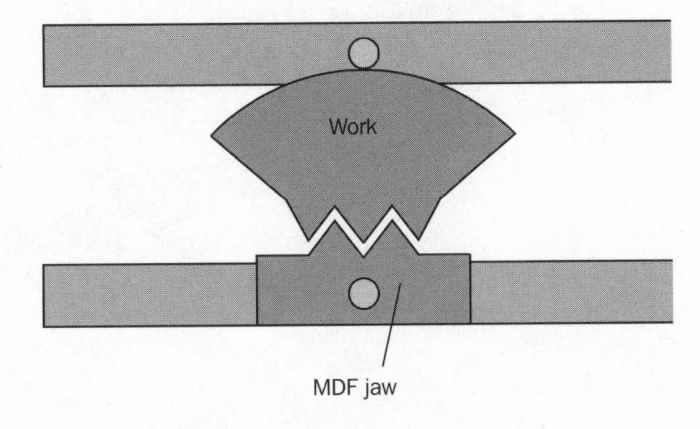

Tommy Restraint

When Lee Dickenson tested the CC2000 workholder from Craft Supplies, he highlighted the problem of losing the tommy bar, a problem which I have eliminated.

I heated one end of the tommy bar until it was red hot then, with the aid of hammer and vice, I flattened the end. I then took the threaded stub (which the tommy bar operates) off the work holder, passed the tommy bar through the stub, heated the other end of the bar and flattened that. This traps the tommy bar in place.

Only a short section of bar needs to be flattened at each end, say about ¼in, 6mm. The amount of distortion need only be enough to form a stop, so you don't have to hammer it very much.

J. Lengthorn

Press Workholder

I made a workholder out of an old Dryad wooden press made for school art departments, probably for bookbinding.

It consists of two jaws and two wooden screw threads which screw into the rear jaw.

I screwed the front jaw to a base board which was wide enough to allow clamping at each end and to a depth of 160mm, 6¼in.

When doing delicate work I staple a piece of old rubber car mat to the jaws.

I have also drilled peg holes in both jaws so I can hold circular or irregular shaped pieces with pegs. The pegs can also hold a base board onto which a block for relief carving can be clamped.

This workholder gives an extra 80mm, 3⅛in height, which can be useful when using a low table.

Frank Biggs

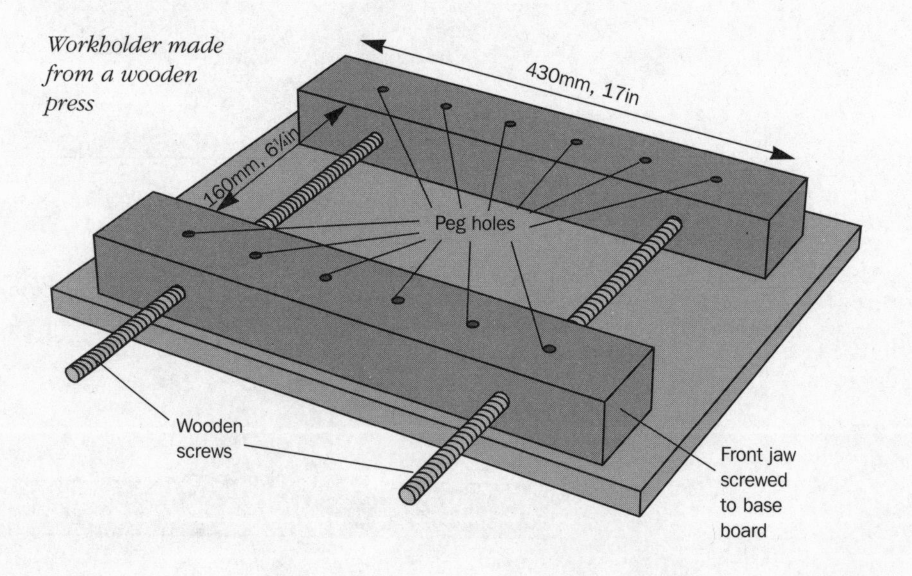

Workholder made from a wooden press

Clamp Aid

Carvers sometimes use F clamps to apply pressure when laminating glued up blocks of wood for carving blanks.

However, those of us who are older, or who have used hand tools for many decades, may find it painful for stiff or arthritic old hands to get sufficient grip and pressure on the long thin clamp handles.

I have made some new handles for my clamps, similar to those on old-fashioned wood braces. They work well and you can grip them sufficiently to apply real pressure.

Remember to always keep the threads of all your clamps well greased.

Clive Price

Home made handle for F clamp

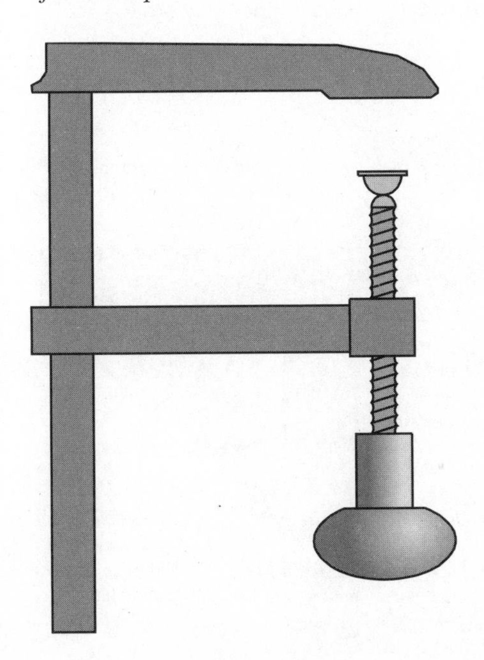

Workmate Wonder

There are many excellent carvers' clamps and workholders on the market, but they can be rather expensive. Here is my idea for a cheap holding device which provides many angles with stability.

I use a Workmate for holding wood, but this can allow the piece to move laterally under pressure. If you overtighten the jaws it can damage the wood.

My workholder is a piece of wood 255 x 50 x 50mm, 10 x 2 x 2in, with slots cut in it either side to fit in the vice jaws.

The slots are 20mm, ¾in, wide x 6mm, ¼in deep and cut parallel to each other about 50mm, 2in in from each end. On one end they are angled at about 30° and at the other end you can cut a different angle to vary the range.

A hole is drilled through the uncut faces about 1½in, 38mm in from each end. This takes a thick wood screw or carvers' screw to hold the workpiece which is simply screwed on.

The holder can be positioned to point either way up or down the Workmate and the workpiece can be fixed above or below the workholder. The workpiece can be revolved by loosening the screw.

The workholder gives increased working height, and can be made longer or shorter to suit your height. The slots enable the Workmate vice jaws to get a really firm grip so the workholder cannot move.

This device has cut down my bad language and increased enormously my pleasure in this satisfying hobby.

Ken Atkins

(See illustration overleaf.)

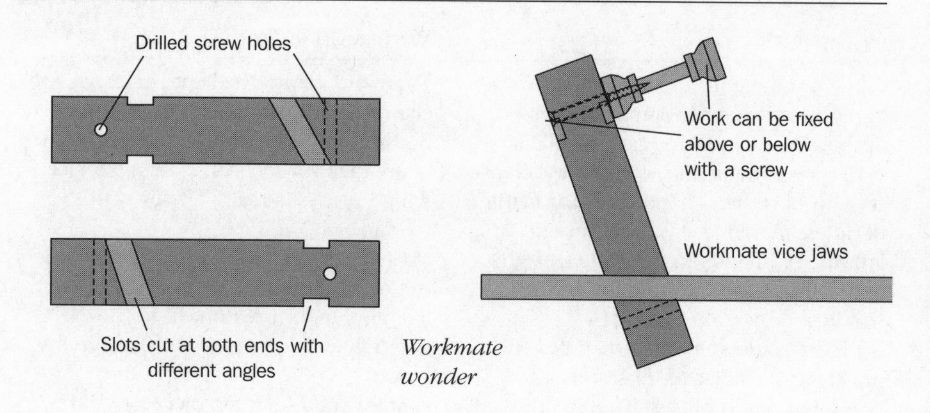

Workmate wonder

Carvers' Screw

When I started carving some years ago, I soon realised that I needed some way of holding down the job and locking it in position. So, I devised my own carvers' screw, without having seen one.

I often use my carvers' screw with what I call my gallows. Made from 50 x 38mm, 2 x 1½in timber, the upright is held in a bench vice to bring the work up to a convenient height. It can also be held at an angle when required.

Sandpaper is glued to the top of the gallows to grip the workpiece securely when the carvers' screw is tightened.

I trust that this idea will help other carvers to keep up the good work.

Bill James Shipwright

Carvers' screw

SIMPLE SUPPORT

Many carvers use elaborate vices, clamps or workholders for carving in the round. For supporting small three-dimensional hand-sized pieces, something that I find works well is a small bag filled with sand, kitty litter, or other small hard grains (even dried beans).

The work is held down on the bag, so that the section being carved is supported. The bag moulds itself to irregular shapes as you carve.

My bag is about 150mm, 6in, square made of soft leather. In twenty years of use I have only had to patch three holes with tape.

E.J. Tangerman

CRAFTY CLAMPING

If you have a Record carvers' clamp and a joiners' bench vice, you can considerably extend the adaptability of the clamp with the use of a wooden extension bar.

First remove the clamps for attaching the device to a bench and insert a wood extension bar of the same section to fit inside the hollow post. The bar is inserted fully into the post and should extend a further 305mm, 12in or so.

Drill two holes in the edge of the post so holding screws can be inserted to secure the extension bar.

Glue rubber chair webbing strips to both sides of the post to give increased grip when the post is held in the vice. Cut holes in the strips to correspond with the holes in the post so the bench clamps can be re-fitted if desired.

Putting the extended clamp in a

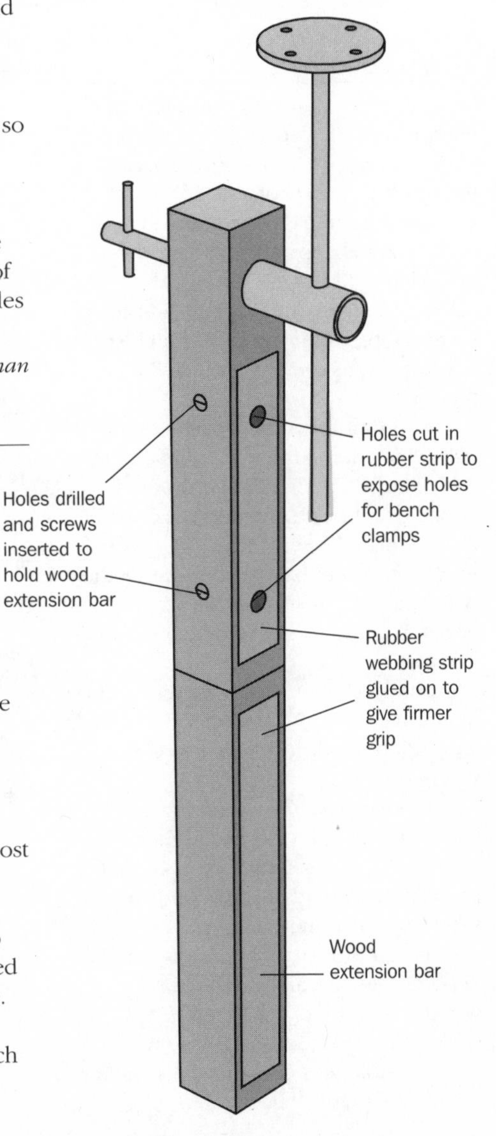

Record carvers' clamp with bench clamps removed

joiners' vice increases its range considerably and is firmer and more stable than using the screw clamps fixed to the edge of a bench.

C. Kelly

Simple Clamping

Sometimes it is necessary to glue on extra pieces of wood to your work, either to remedy a mistake or because the finished piece consists of carved elements that must be assembled.

Ordinary clamps and holding devices are usually designed more for the cabinetmaker than the carver and may be no help, and many of the high-speed adhesives create more problems than they solve.

I have found two invaluable clamping aids which are extremely adaptable to odd shapes. The first is the ordinary elastic or rubber band, such as used by the postman. They can be adjusted to hold almost any pair of shapes together, with suitable pads or blocks where necessary, and can provide considerable pressure.

If one side of an assembly tends to be pulled by the bands you can rotate them around the work to put more tension where it belongs.

The other device is taken from Grinling Gibbons who used brads, or small nails, to assemble his work. The problem with brads is they leave a hole where you may not want it.

I find an ordinary straight pin can be driven in like a nail to bark or soft wood. It will hold just as well, and when withdrawn leaves a hole which is hardly visible and does not need filling.

E.J. Tangerman

Holding Relief

I have found that when holding low relief carving work, clamps often vibrate loose. Clamps are also particularly dangerous during machining operations: accidental contact of power tool and clamp does neither any good and could result in injury to the carver. The two methods that I frequently use follow.

Double sided sticky tape. I use a thin tape with a high 'tack'; in other words it grips well. Thick tapes allow the carving to vibrate under pressure from the tools, which makes accuracy difficult. Double sided tape is the sort of thing used to hold down vinyl flooring or in cheaper double glazing units.

Holt-melt glue. Many people have written about using hot-melt glue to hold work, most simply use spots of hot-melt glue underneath the work to hold it in place. I don't recommend that you put any glue underneath, as I found it difficult to get the work off its backing, and you get problems with vibration. I use a bead of hot-melt glue around the outer edge of the work. This way it can easily be cut off its backing after carving.

I use both the above methods to hold carvings on to a larger backing of scrap plywood, which can be held to the bench by a number of other methods.

Rod Naylor

Cheap Clamp

I made a cheap woodcarvers' clamp with an old sink waste pipe and securing nut, a 150 x 12mm, 6 x ½in, bolt with its head cut off and two nuts, a small metal plate about 75mm, 3in, diameter and a block of hardwood.

The hardwood block is drilled through to take the sink waste pipe as a sliding fit. The waste pipe is drilled through to take the bolt, and the assembly is held by tightening the waste pipe nut.

The metal plate is drilled to take the bolt, which is secured by two nuts, and there are other holes drilled in the plate to take securing screws for the workpiece.

You will also need a piece of wood on top of the plate, the same thickness as the nut, and drilled to take the nut and screw holes.

The wood block can be held in a vice or clamped to a bench. I can get a full 360° rotation in any plane.

W.T. Miles

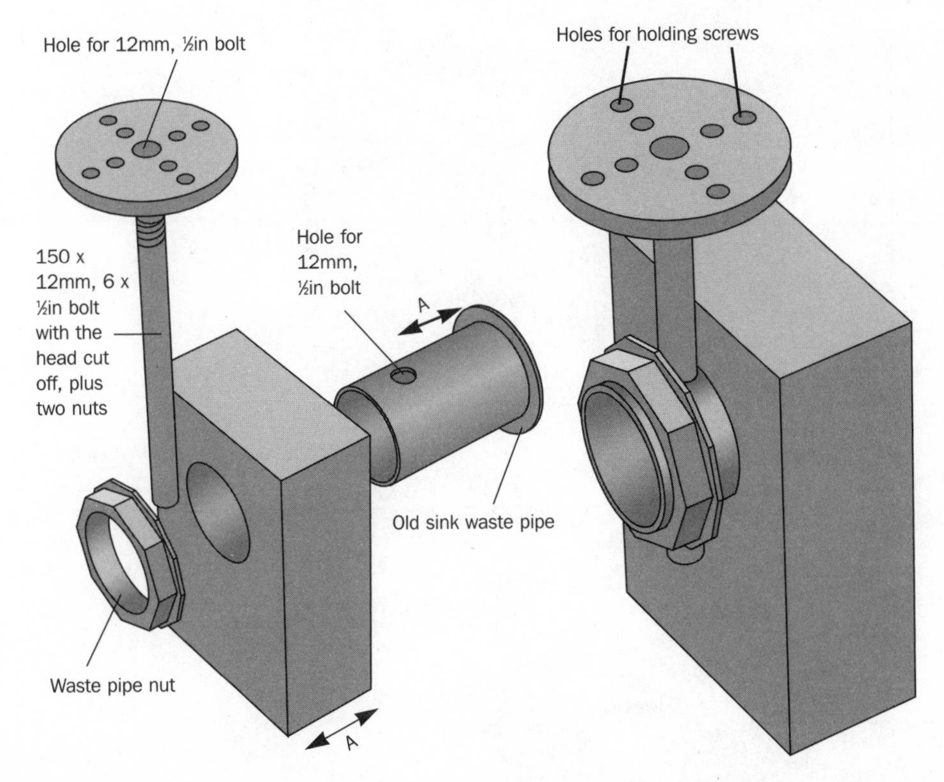

Cheap clamp

Portable Work Centre

If you have a workshop with a bench, you can do relief carving using vices or bench dogs to hold the work.

However, if you are like me you may often carve when and where the mood strikes you, such as on a park bench, in an easy chair watching TV, or at the kitchen table. In that case you will need something portable to hold the wood.

This simple, portable relief carving work centre system I have devised will secure boards of various sizes securely for relief carving wherever I happen to be.

The device has worked well for me, and I am sure readers could adapt it to suit their needs.

R.B. Himes

Portable work centre

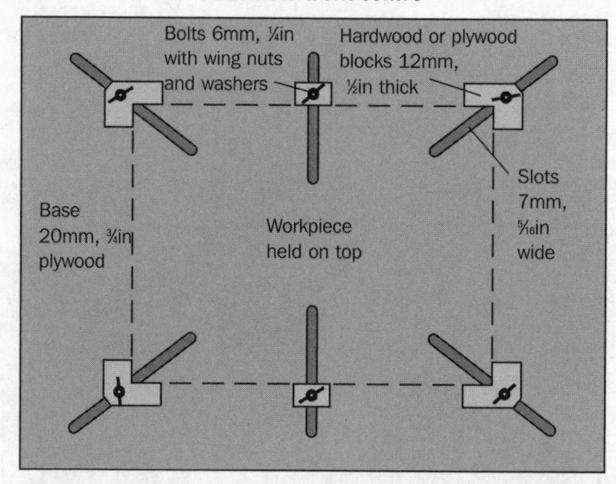

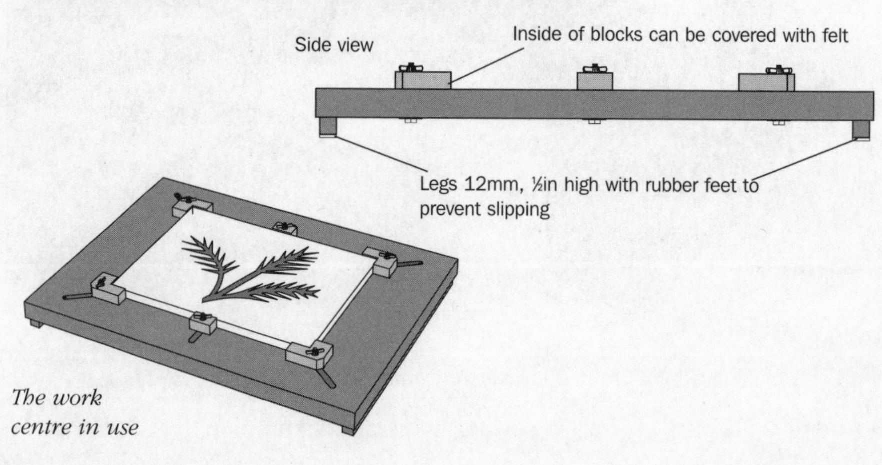

The work centre in use

Section 5
WOOD

Woodworm Trap

Here's an idea for protecting your valuable timber store from woodworm. Sapwood from English walnut *(Juglans regia)* is caviar to the woodworm. If you don't have any walnut then beech *(Fagus sylvatica)* is a reasonably good second choice.

Prepare some pieces with a rough sawn surface, preferably lightly pulped with a hammer. This will prove an irresistible starting point for the grubs to start nibbling.

If you place some such pieces around your wood store it will attract the adult beetles to lay their eggs. English woodworm usually have a three year life cycle, so if you burn the pieces at the end of the second summer you should destroy two years' eggs, and help protect your good timber.

Rod Naylor

Hiding Cracks

Many large logs have checks (shakes or cracks) from drying stresses. In some cases these checks occur at very undesirable places in a carving. The usual remedy is to attempt to push in a glue and sawdust mixture, which usually doesn't penetrate.

I have found it better to put the glue on alone, work it down into the check with a thin-bladed knife, then sprinkle the area with sawdust and work that in turn. The result is a crevice that is more deeply filled.

Larger breaks or imperfections in the wood should be filled with pieces of the same wood, carefully fitted, because a sawdust-filled hole of any size will have a different colour, even before finishing. I usually make such repairs with a filler piece cut carefully from a chip of the same colour and grain direction as the wood around the flaw.

E.J. Tangerman

Bargain Boards

Buying seasoned wood blanks for relief carving can be prohibitively expensive, especially for those on low incomes. I have found a good source of cheap blanks to be jumble sales, car boot sales and the like where you can pick up old wooden bread or other cutting boards (preferably beech) of various sizes and thicknesses often for only a few pence each. Cleaned and sanded, these make ideal carving blanks.

P. Vardigans

Waste Wood

Demolition contractors' and builders' yards have been good places to find all types of wood over the years. Second-hand furniture shops and auction sales have also proved successful hunting grounds.

Such opportunities are not now as

plentiful as they were. However, many timber yards acquiesce to a polite enquiry requesting permission to inspect the offcuts in the waste bin. Precious material can be gained for your hobby, usually for the price of a cheery 'Thank-you'.

Gordon Wagstaff

Keep it Covered

It is a good idea to keep wood being carved in a plastic bag except when you are actually working, especially in warm weather. This is because wood warps continuously as temperature and humidity change, and this is especially so when wood is being worked.

A plastic bag slows the drying and helps to prevent splitting. Water will still pass through the plastic, but at a much slower rate. When carving wet wood in warm weather, I wet the wood before putting it in the plastic.

It is particularly important to keep work covered after using a copying machine. If you don't you can find work will have warped or shrunk so much that you cannot carve in fine detail.

Rod Naylor

SECTION 6
SANDING

DRUM SANDER

Thread one 5mm, 3⁄16in washer on to the bolt, followed by a number of tap washers until you have a pile of washers equal to the width of the Velcro. End with a 3⁄16in, 5mm washer and two nuts.

Measure the circumference of the sanding drum and cut a strip of Velcro to suit, then several pieces of felt backed abrasive to match. Stick the Velcro around the drum then an abrasive strip can be fixed to the Velcro – making sure that the join of the abrasive is not in the same place as the join in the Velcro. Tighten the first nut against the tap washers then lock it with the second nut. You are now equipped with a sanding drum.

A. Withers

SANDING TIP

I often roll a piece of cloth-backed abrasive around a wooden dowel, when sanding a carving – the size of the dowel is determined by the size of the piece you're working on. I also glue bits of abrasive on to small sticks or tongue depressors, giving me a range of fine rifflers for finishing. But, for small deep areas I use another trick.

Take a nail, cut the head off and round off the pointed end. Put double-sided adhesive tape round the nail, then wind steel wool round the tape. With this nail in a power tool you have an excellent, and quite strong little sander. Remember to wear safety goggles when using this sander, as it may disintegrate if you get too enthusiastic.

Margaret Cawood

Drum Sander

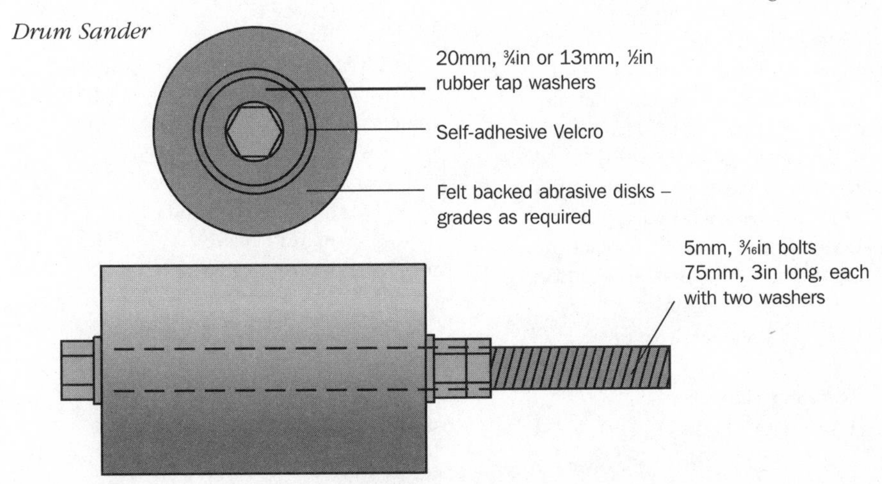

Sanding Flat

With increasing problems of failing eyesight and arthritis, I am constantly trying to lessen wear and tear on my joints and my sight, particularly when carving. One of the most frustrating things for me, was trying to obtain a flat, level base on my small carvings, and at times making straight edges. Inspiration came to the rescue.

When the surface of my Sandvik sandplate was worn out I ordered two replacements – one to fit on my old handle, the other to stick directly on to the top of my small workbench, in one corner. To sand the base of my pieces I rub them on the sandplate, rather than the other way round, it is also easy to get straight edges this way.

I also have a mobile version, which is made with worn sandplates. They are stuck with double-sided adhesive tape on to a piece of flat wood, about 50mm, 2in longer than the plate, leaving 25mm, an inch of wood showing at both ends. When demonstrating at local events, I clamp this portable, rigid, non-tearing sander to the table with two G-clamps.

Another trick – this time with the Sandvik sandplate on the original handle – is to clamp the sandplate handle in the bench vice at an angle. This enables me to see more easily some of the awkward angles of my carvings, when sanding.

Other readers, who suffer from glaucoma, might like to contact the International Glaucoma Association (IGA). The IGA's address is:
IGA, Kings College Hospital,
Denmark Hill,
London SE5 9RS
Enclose a SAE if you expect a reply.

Patricia Vardigans

Softer Sanding

With summer over, here's a use for those worn out old flip-flops; use them as backing pads for sanding blocks.

Blocks made just from wood are normally too rigid to be used on carvings as they force you to sand away any high detail. But high density foam such as that used for packing, or flip-flop soles, is excellent as it flexes round the curves and gives a softer finish.

Flip-flop soles are about the right density but are usually too thin. Try gluing a pair together or on to a wooden backing.

The same foam can also be used as clamp blocks when gluing up irregularly-shaped work.

Rod Naylor

Handy Sander

For sanding in small places and difficult corners I use an old hacksaw blade with Sandvik Sandplate stuck on.

The hacksaw blade is ground to the shape required and has a hole drilled on one end so it can be hung up when not in use.

Sandplate is available in two grades and two sizes from DIY stores. Cut it to match the shape of the blade with tinsnips.

The material has an adhesive backing which you just stick to the blade. I find it holds well and makes an excellent tool which I use regularly.

E. Ward

Flexible Sanders

As a newcomer to woodcarving with only a few tools, no mechanical aids, and little experience of tackling difficult parts of carvings, I sometimes have to develop my own methods to overcome problems.

One such area is sanding curved areas at the finishing stages of a carving. I have found flexible sanding strips most useful for this.

I make the strips by sticking pieces of different grades of abrasive papers on to fabric strips with contact adhesive. The abrasive strips are 12-20mm, ½-¾in wide x 200mm, 8in long, and the fabric strips 20-25mm, ¾-1in wide x 305mm, 12in long. The fabric strip is about 6mm, ¼in wider than the abrasive to ensure the area being sanded is not marked by the edge of the abrasive.

You can put different grades of abrasive on each side of a fabric strip, and the fabric should be stretched slightly while applying the glued paper so it does not wrinkle.

I found the best fabric was the hem of an old sheet. The sheet tore easily along the hem and left a strip 25mm, 1in wide, double thickness and strong yet soft.

The fabric backing gives greater strength to the strip of abrasive, prevents the paper tearing, and prolongs its useful life.

Holding a strip with both hands, it can be used to smooth areas of a carving to a fine finish. The strips are particularly useful for areas where access is restricted, for fine shaping of double curvature areas, and for small adjustments to some muscle and bone structures.

T.G. Laidler

SECTION 7
GENERAL

WARMER WORKSHOP

I know many people like me use a garden shed as a workshop, and they can be cold, damp and draughty in winter. My own workshop was 3 x 2.4m, 10 x 8ft and lap boarded.

I insulated it with glass fibre and hardboard and improved the door to keep out draughts, but it was still cold and damp in winter allowing tools to rust and timber to swell.

Trying to carve a delicate piece wrapped in a thick coat and gloves while stamping your feet is not pleasant, so when I got another shed to add to my existing one I used 12mm, ½in chipboard offcuts to insulate it.

I also installed electricity and two tubular heaters with a total output of just 300W. I kept these on continuously and have been impressed by their efficiency and low running cost over the past two winters.

I have had no more problems with damp or cold. I keep some matches on my bench to test for damp, and they invariably strike.

If the temperature outside is above freezing, no further heat is required.

One note of warning, never use paraffin heaters as they produce more moisture than they burn.

Basil Coates

PAPER POINTER

Finding the right grade of abrasive paper among the workshop shavings and sawdust can be a problem. Whole sheets are coded with their grit numbers, but when cut into strips it is easy enough to confuse the grades, especially if they are all the same colour.

It can be very frustrating if you pick up the wrong grade by mistake and find you are sanding with a coarse grit when you have already got down to a fine cut.

I usually work with three grades of abrasive at any time, and I avoid confusion by cutting the ends of the strips to identify the grades. For example, coarse grades are cut straight across, medium grades have the ends cut diagonally left to right and fine grades from right to left.

If working with more than three grades you can cut notches as well.

Jeremy Williams

OLD GLOVES

Like many of my generation I hate to throw things away when there is some use left in them. Any keen gardener, like me, is likely to get through plenty of work gloves. Mine never go to waste if they have any leather in them. I retrieve the soft suede leather as it is ideal for ➢

many jobs, for example: edge tool protection, stropping, or simply wiping off oil when honing.

P.R. Griffiths

Filing

This is not an earth-shattering tip, but you may find it helpful. When I read through *Woodcarving* magazine I come across lots of bits and pieces that might come in useful 'one day'. And there are lovely photographs of carvings I might like to refer to, or I may want information from one of the tool tests.

I am sure that many have had the experience of wanting to refer to something useful from an old *Woodcarving* magazine, but having to leaf through a pile of them because we can't quite remember which one it was in. This has its uses, as I have come across things I had forgotten about.

However, I find that a sticky label on the corner of the magazine cover, with page number and subjects of interest noted down, is useful for quick reference.

Vera Feldman

Spot Fakes

Old woodcarvings can be valuable, and I have come across some fakes. Here are some tips for spotting fakers' mistakes.

Dowels used to joint sections together were not circular before the 1790s when drill bits were developed to drill round holes. Early joints were more like nailed construction, but using wooden nails.

Circular saw marks will not be on wood before 1830, and router marks from a carving machine not before 1835.

Ripples running across the grain, as made by a planing machine, are unusual before 1850. Although developed earlier than this, they are not normally found until after 1900.

Marks which appear to have been made by a bandsaw can cause confusion as they may have been made by a frame saw, a machine in common use since the late 1600s and developed even earlier.

Woodworm usually make a series of round holes of varying sizes. They should penetrate into the wood for only about 2mm before changing direction and running along beneath the surface.

Woodworm are grubs which live in the wood for several years. They change into beetles before eating their way out to lay more eggs.

When woodworm marks appear as a series of irregular channels on the surface, it is often because an old beam or large piece of scrap was subsequently carved.

If the wood was heavily painted or gilded the woodworm would have a false idea of where the surface was and stripping would reveal the channels.

Rod Naylor

Pack a Purse

It is all too easy to lose small items in the workshop, screws, nuts, Allen keys, drill bits, small burrs and so on.

One solution to this is to use cheap nylon wrist purses. These are about 75 x 50mm, 3 x 2in with a zip and Velcro strap.

These can be fastened round your wrist, to toolbox handles, or fixed points in the workshop. I keep power tool chuck keys and spanners in a purse fixed to the tool's power cable.

These purses are available from charity and gift shops, or you can make your own from leather scraps, glue, and Velcro strip from a sewing shop.
You can also use photographic film containers with Velcro strip glued on, or drill two holes in the container and tie it on.

John Beart

Lap Board

High-tech lap-top computers are all the rage these days, but my lap-top carving board uses very low-tech materials and ideas for a satisfactory and low-cost result.

All I used were an old, very thick, square bread board, an old, unwanted leather belt, two screws and two washers.

I cut the belt into two lengths, one-third along from the buckle end. Then I punched holes through the belt a short way in from each of the cut ends. I drilled screw holes in either side of the board, a short distance from the ends, and screwed the belt sections to the board, using the washers to protect the belt from the screw heads.

The belt, when fastened round my waist, prevents the board/carving table from slipping off my lap and can also be used as a shoulder strap for carrying the board around easily.

P. Vardigans

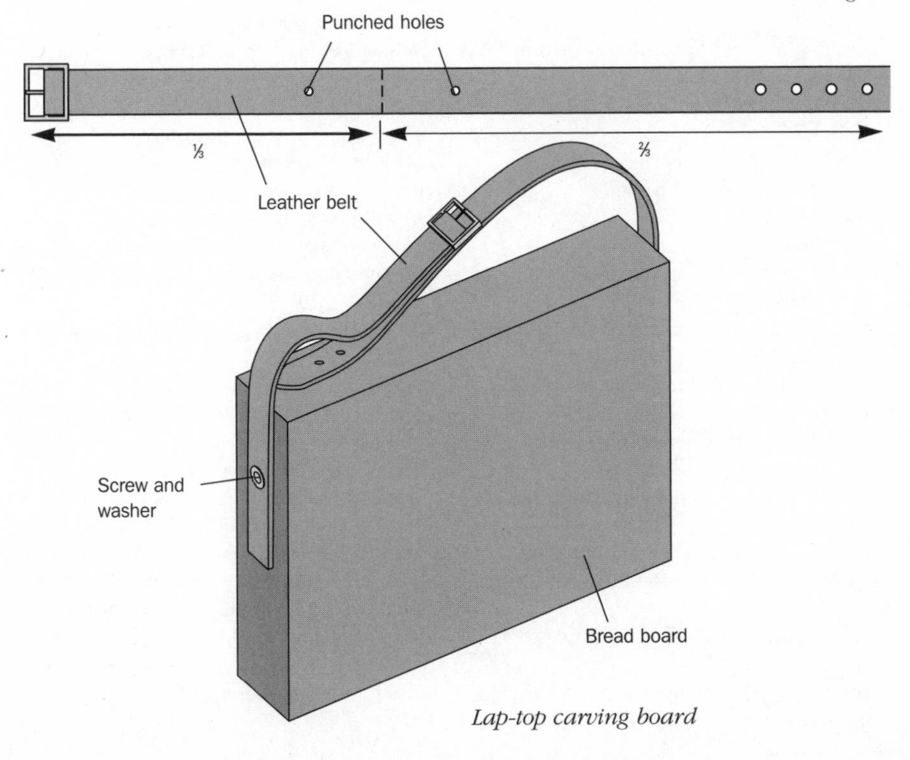

Lap-top carving board

INDEX

A
abrafile blades, made into rifflers 12
abrasive papers
  coding for grades 45
  used with carvers' screws to grip work 34
acetate film, used as a guide for relief carving 19–20
angle grinders
  overcoming clogged on/off switches 6
  used to speed up copying machines 21
awkward shapes, held in adapted vice 31

B
baseball gloves, used to protect fingers when sanding 15
bean bags, used to hold work 35
benches
  extra bench to give correct height 22
  made to the correct height 21
  non-slip surface for 28
birds, carved
  holder for painting 28
  jig for making wire feet 29–30
bookbinding presses, adapted as workholders 32
bow-saw blades, making your own 7
boxes for carving tools
  made from corrugated roofing 6
  made from record cases 12–13
bread boards, used as cheap blanks for relief carving 39
bullnosing gouges and firmer chisels 7

C
carvers' clamps, made from sink waste pipes 37
carvers' cramps, making extension bars for 35–6
carvers' screws, making your own 34
carving boards, portable, making 47
carving jig for making thin sheets of wood 23–4
carving tools
  avoiding breakages to 25
  colour coding handles 12–13
  making boxes for 6, 12–13
  making leather guards for 14
chalk, as a guide for carved lettering 19
checks, filling with glue and sawdust 39
chisels
  made from putty & scribing knives 5
  miniature, made from dentists' tools 3
  miniature, made from masonry nails 14
  miniature, made from needle files 14
  preventing damage from ferrules 6–7
chuck keys, keeping safe 46–7
circular cutters, made from keys 11
clamp blocks, made from flip-flops 42
colour coding carving tool handles 12–13
computers, as an aid to designing carved lettering 19
coping saw, used for preliminary shaping 25
copper pipe, used as a mallet 3
copy carving, device to aid marking up 20
copy carving machines
  increasing cutting speed 21
  need to prevent warping when using 40
  used to speed up cutting low reliefs 21
corrugated roofing, made into boxes for carving tools 6
cracks, filling with glue and sawdust 39
current breaker, residual, used as a safety measure 4
cut-off tools, sharpening 17

D

delicate carvings, held with hot melt glue 22
dentists' tools, using 3–4
depth gauges for relief carvings, making 8–9
double-sided tape, used to hold relief work for machining 36
drill bits, keeping safe 46–7
drum sanders, making your own 41

E

emery boards, used to sand in awkward corners 12
eyes, in wildlife subjects, making 11
eyesight problems, overcoming 4–5, 42

F

fake carvings, spotting 46
F-clamps, making larger handles for 33
ferrules, preventing damage from 6–7
firmer chisels, bullnose grinding 7
flexible shaft carving machines
 avoiding shaft damage 4
 used to sand deep undercuts 8
flexible strips for sanding, making 43
flip-flops, used as sanding pads & clamp blocks 42
fretwork panels, faster carving using a copying machine 21

G

gallows stand for holding carvings, making 30
gloves, leather
 used to protect fingers when sanding 15
 uses for old 45–6
golfers' gloves, used to protect fingers when sanding 15
gouges
 bent, problems with when using mallets 25
 bullnose grinding 7
 colour coding for sweeps 12–13
 miniature, made from dentists' tools 3
 miniature, made from umbrella spines 14
 preventing damage from ferrules 6–7
 sharpening 17

H

hacksaw blades
 adapted as tools 13, 42
 using in tight corners 7
high density foam, used as non-slip surface for workbench 28
hot melt glue
 cleaning up 23
 overcoming problems of using on metal 23
 used to hold low relief work for machining 36
 used to hold small carvings 22

J

jammed tools, removing 25
jigs
 for thin sheets of wood 24–5
 for wire feet for carved birds 29–30

K

keys, adapted as circular cutters 11

L

large carvings, workholder for 27
leather guards for carving tools, making 14
lettering, carved
 obtaining correct layout using a computer 19
 roughing out in chalk 19
low relief carving, faster cutting with a copying machine 21

M

macaronis, sharpening 17
magazines, carving, indexing interesting articles 46
mallets
 made from copper pipe 3
 making your own 3, 10–11
 rubber, used to cut noise & jarring 5
 to fit the hand 10–11
 used correctly with bent gouges 25

masonry nails, adapted as miniature chisels 14
miniature tools
chisels, made from masonry nails 14
chisels, made from needle files 14
gouges, made from umbrella spines 14
made from dentists' tools 3

N

nail sculpture novelties, used as profile gauges 15
needle files, adapted as miniature chisels 14

P

padsaws adapted for hacksaw blades 7
painting carved birds, holder for 28
panic switch for power tools 4
parting tools, sharpening 17
photographic film cases, used for storing oddments 46–7
pins, used as clamping aids when gluing 36
portable workholders, making 38
power tools
angle grinders, overcoming clogged on/off switches 6
safety measures 4
profile gauges, nail sculpture novelties used as 15
purses, used for storing oddments 46–7
push cuts versus pull cuts when using saws 25
putty knives converted to chisels 5

R

rasps, made from sintered metal abrasive 9–10
reading glasses used for detail work 4–5
record cases, made into boxes for carving tools 12–13
relief carving
acetate film used as a guide 19–20
cheap blanks from bread boards 39
faster cutting with copy carving machines 21
holding with double-sided tape 36
holding with hot melt glue 36
making depth gauges for 8–9
residual current breaker, used as a safety measure 4
rifflers
made from abrafile blades 12
made from hacksaw blades 13
made from sintered metal abrasive 9–10
made from tungsten carbide sheet 21–2
miniature, made from dentists' tools 3
rubber bands, used as clamping aids when gluing 36

S

safety measures
residual current breaker 4
thumb shields 5, 10
when using blowtorches 23
sandbags, used to hold work 35
sanding
deep undercuts 8
flat surfaces 42
for a zit-free surface 24
in awkward corners, with emery boards 12
in awkward corners, with Sandvik Sandplate 42
in awkward corners, with steel wool 41
with flexible strips 43
without sore fingertips 15
sanding blocks, made from flip-flops 42
sanding drums, making your own 41
sanding machines, used to make thin sheets of wood 23–4
sanding sealer, used to ease removal of hot melt glue 23
sandpaper
coding for grades 45
used with carvers' screws to grip work 34
Sandvik Sandplate, sanding in awkward corners with 42
sash cramps, used to modify workholders 27
saws, made for tight corners 7

scorps, made from shave hooks 11–12
scrapers
made from hacksaw blades 13
made from shave hooks 11–12
scratches on white painted wood, hiding 24
scribing knives converted to chisels 5
shakes, filling with glue and sawdust 39
sharpening
V-tools 17
shave hooks, used as scrapers 11–12
sintered metal abrasive, made into rasps & rifflers 9–10
small carvings, held with hot melt glue 22
spectacles, reading, used for detail work 4–5
splitting, preventing 19
stand for holding carvings, making 30
steel wool, used to sand in awkward corners 41

T

thin sheets of wood, carving jig for 23–4
thumb shields
made from fingerstalls 10
made from plastic pipe 5
timber
cheap sources of 39–40
hiding cracks in 39
protecting against woodworm 39
protecting from warping 40
tommy bar for CC2000 workholder, preventing loss 32
tools, carving
avoiding breakages to 25
colour coding handles 12–13
making boxes for 6, 12–13
making leather guards for 14
transferring designs to a block 20–1

U

umbrella spines, adapted as miniature gouges 14

V

vices, adapted to hold awkward shapes 31
V-tools, sharpening 17

W

wildlife subjects, making eyes for 11
woodworm, protecting timber from 39
workbenches
extra bench to give correct height 22
made to the correct height 21
non-slip surface for 28
workholders
adapted with sash cramps 27
CC2000, preventing loss of tommy bar 32
for large blocks 27
gallows stand, making 30
made from bookbinding presses 32
made from Workmate 33–4
portable 38
vices adapted to hold awkward shapes 31
Workmates, adapted as workholders 33–4
workpieces, gluing on extra sections 36
workshops, warming in winter 45

Z

zits, overcoming on polished carvings 24

TITLES AVAILABLE FROM GMC PUBLICATIONS

BOOKS

WOODTURNING

Adventures in Woodturning	*David Springett*
Bert Marsh: Woodturner	*Bert Marsh*
Bill Jones' Notes from the Turning Shop	*Bill Jones*
Bill Jones' Further Notes from the Turning Shop	*Bill Jones*
Carving on Turning	*Chris Pye*
Colouring Techniques for Woodturners	*Jan Sanders*
Decorative Techniques for Woodturners	*Hilary Bowen*
Faceplate Turning: Features, Projects, Practice	*GMC Publications*
Green Woodwork	*Mike Abbott*
Illustrated Woodturning Techniques	*John Hunnex*
Keith Rowley's Woodturning Projects	*Keith Rowley*
Make Money from Woodturning	*Ann & Bob Phillips*
Multi-Centre Woodturning	*Ray Hopper*
Pleasure & Profit from Woodturning	*Reg Sherwin*
Practical Tips for Turners & Carvers	*GMC Publications*
Practical Tips for Woodturners	*GMC Publications*
Spindle Turning	*GMC Publications*
Turning Miniatures in Wood	*John Sainsbury*
Turning Wooden Toys	*Terry Lawrence*
Understanding Woodturning	*Ann & Bob Phillips*
Useful Woodturning Projects	*GMC Publications*
Woodturning: A Foundation Course	*Keith Rowley*
Woodturning Jewellery	*Hilary Bowen*
Woodturning Masterclass	*Tony Boase*
Woodturning: A Source Book of Shapes	*John Hunnex*
Woodturning Techniques	*GMC Publications*
Woodturning Wizardry	*David Springett*

WOODCARVING

The Art of the Woodcarver	*GMC Publications*
Carving Birds & Beasts	*GMC Publications*
Carving Realistic Birds	*David Tippey*
Carving on Turning	*Chris Pye*
Decorative Woodcarving	*Jeremy Williams*
Essential Woodcarving Techniques	*Dick Onians*
Lettercarving in Wood	*Chris Pye*
Practical Tips for Turners & Carvers	*GMC Publications*
Understanding Woodcarving	*GMC Publication*
Wildfowl Carving Volume 1	*Jim Pearce*
Wildfowl Carving Volume 2	*Jim Pearce*
The Woodcarvers	*GMC Publications*
Woodcarving: A Complete Course	*Ron Butterfield*
Woodcarving for Beginners: Projects, Techniques & Tools	*GMC Publications*
Woodcarving Tools, Materials & Equipment	*Chris Pye*

PLANS, PROJECTS, TOOLS & THE WORKSHOP

The Incredible Router	*Jeremy Broun*
Making & Modifying Woodworking Tools	*Jim Kingshott*
Sharpening: The Complete Guide	*Jim Kingshott*
Sharpening Pocket Reference Book	*Jim Kingshott*
The Workshop	*Jim Kingshott*

TOYS & MINIATURES	Designing & Making Wooden Toys	*Terry Kelly*
	Fun to Make Wooden Toys & Games	*Jeff & Jennie Loader*
	Making Wooden Toys & Games	*Jeff & Jennie Loader*
	Making Board, Peg & Dice Games	*Jeff & Jennie Loader*
	Making Little Boxes from Wood	*John Bennett*
	Miniature Needlepoint Carpets	*Janet Granger*
	Turning Miniatures in Wood	*John Sainsbury*
	Turning Wooden Toys	*Terry Lawrence*
CREATIVE CRAFTS	Celtic Knotwork Designs	*Sheila Sturrock*
	Collage from Seeds, Leaves and Flowers	*Joan Carver*
	The Complete Pyrography	*Stephen Poole*
	Creating Knitwear Designs	*Pat Ashforth & Steve Plummer*
	Cross Stitch on Colour	*Sheena Rogers*
	Embroidery Tips & Hints	*Harold Hayes*
	Making Knitwear Fit	*Pat Ashforth & Steve Plummer*
	Miniature Needlepoint Carpets	*Janet Granger*
	Tatting Collage	*Lindsay Rogers*
UPHOLSTERY & FURNITURE	Care & Repair	*GMC Publications*
	Complete Woodfinishing	*Ian Hosker*
	Woodfinishing Handbook (Practical Crafts)	*Ian Hosker*
	Furniture Projects	*Rod Wales*
	Furniture Restoration (Practical Crafts)	*Kevin Jan Bonner*
	Furniture Restoration & Repair for Beginners	*Kevin Jan Bonner*
	Green Woodwork	*Mike Abbott*
	Making Fine Furniture	*Tom Darby*
	Making Shaker Furniture	*Barry Jackson*
	Pine Furniture Projects	*Dave Mackenzie*
	Seat Weaving (Practical Crafts)	*Ricky Holdstock*
	Upholsterer's Pocket Reference Book	*David James*
	Upholstery: A Complete Course	*David James*
	Upholstery: Techniques & Projects	*David James*
DOLLS' HOUSES & DOLLS' HOUSE FURNITURE	Architecture for Dolls' Houses	*Joyce Percival*
	A Beginners' Guide to the Dolls' House Hobby	*Jean Nisbett*
	The Complete Dolls' House Book	*Jean Nisbett*
	Easy-to-Make Dolls' House Accessories	*Andrea Barham*
	Make Your Own Dolls' House Furniture	*Maurice Harper*
	Making Dolls' House Furniture	*Patricia King*
	Making Period Dolls' House Accessories	*Andrea Barham*
	Making Period Dolls' House Furniture	*Derek & Sheila Rowbottom*
	Making Victorian Dolls' House Furniture	*Patricia King*
	Miniature Needlepoint Carpets	*Janet Granger*
	The Secrets of the Dolls' House Makers	*Jean Nisbett*
OTHER BOOKS	Guide to Marketing	*GMC Publications*
	Woodworkers' Career & Educational Source Book	*GMC Publications*